First World War
and Army of Occupation
War Diary
France, Belgium and Germany

14 DIVISION
42 Infantry Brigade,
Brigade Trench Mortar Battery
28 July 1915 - 31 August 1916

WO95/1902/4

The Naval & Military Press Ltd
www.nmarchive.com
Published in association with The National Archives

Published by

The Naval & Military Press Ltd

Unit 10 Ridgewood Industrial Park,

Uckfield, East Sussex,

TN22 5QE England

Tel: +44 (0) 1825 749494

www.naval-military-press.com

www.nmarchive.com

This diary has been reprinted in facsimile from the original. Any imperfections are inevitably reproduced and the quality may fall short of modern type and cartographic standards.

© **Crown Copyright**
Images reproduced by permission of The National Archives, London, England, 2015.

Contents

Document type	Place/Title	Date From	Date To
Heading	14 Div 42 Bde 42 Trench Mortar Bty		
War Diary	In The Field	01/08/1915	07/08/1915
War Diary	Sheet 28 N.W. B 29a 34	08/08/1915	14/08/1915
War Diary	In The Field	15/08/1915	21/08/1915
War Diary	Breilen	22/08/1915	28/08/1915
War Diary	In The Field	28/07/1915	01/11/1915
War Diary	I. 10. C.9.3	02/11/1915	04/11/1915
War Diary	In The Field	05/11/1915	06/11/1915
War Diary	I.10.C.9.3		
War Diary	Reference Sheet 2 36 N.W. C.25.C.3.2	07/11/1915	13/11/1915
War Diary	36 N.W. Sheet C.25.C.3.2	14/11/1915	20/11/1915
War Diary	10.B.5.5	21/11/1915	21/11/1915
War Diary	11.C.3.5	22/11/1915	22/11/1915
War Diary	10.B.5.5	23/11/1915	23/11/1915
War Diary	10.C.5.6		
War Diary	10.B.5.5	24/11/1915	27/11/1915
War Diary	21 Div.	29/11/1915	15/12/1915
War Diary	21st Division Trenches No 67 To 73	12/12/1915	23/12/1915
War Diary	21st Division Trenches No 67 To 73	23/12/1915	31/12/1915
Heading	42 Trench Motar Bty Jan Vol II		
War Diary	I 10 d 1.2	01/01/1916	31/01/1916
War Diary	I 10 d 1.2	01/02/1916	29/02/1916
Heading	42/1 T. Howitzer Battery March 1916		
War Diary	Simencourt	02/03/1916	02/03/1916
War Diary	Arras	09/03/1916	31/03/1916
War Diary	Arras	01/04/1916	28/04/1916
Heading	42/2 T M Bty March 16 Vol 1 & 2		
War Diary	Arras	06/04/1916	30/04/1916
Heading	42/1 TM Bty Vol 3		
War Diary	Arras	06/04/1916	06/05/1916
War Diary	Arras	01/05/1916	13/05/1916
War Diary	Arras	07/05/1916	17/05/1916
War Diary	Arras	14/05/1916	26/05/1916
War Diary	Arras	18/05/1916	31/05/1916
War Diary	Arras	27/05/1916	31/05/1916
Heading	42/2 TM Bty Vol 3		
War Diary	Arras	01/05/1916	31/05/1916
War Diary	Arras	01/05/1916	30/06/1916
Heading	42/2 T M Bty Vol 4		
War Diary	Arras	01/06/1916	30/06/1916
Heading	42/1 TM Bty Vol 4		
War Diary	Arras	01/06/1916	19/06/1916
Heading	War Diary Of 42nd Trench Mortar Battery 1st-31st July 1916		
War Diary	Arras	01/07/1916	31/07/1916
Heading	War Diary Secret 42nd Trench Mortar Battery. 1st-31st August Vol. 6		
War Diary	Fienvillers	01/08/1916	07/08/1916
War Diary	Buire-Sur-L'Ancre	08/08/1916	11/08/1916
War Diary	Reference Albert Combined Sheet F.14.b	12/08/1916	18/08/1916

War Diary	Montauban And In Line In Delville Wood	19/08/1916	20/08/1916
War Diary	Delville Wood	21/08/1916	25/08/1916
War Diary	Bivouac F.14. B. Combined Sheet Albert	26/08/1916	31/08/1916

2 ~~ARTY TROOPS~~

(14 DIV 42 Bde)

42

TRENCH MORTAR

BTY

1915 AUG to 1916 AUG

~~1596~~

WAR DIARY
or
INTELLIGENCE SUMMARY

Army Form C. 2118

1/9th T.H. Kent

Place	Date	Hour	Summary of Events and Information	Remarks and references to Appendices
In the field	1.8.15		In the afternoon the enemy opened fire with their mortars. We replied with five heavy bombs, four of which detonated, the damage done being considerable.	
	2.8.15	At 2.45 am	the enemy began throwing hand grenades over into our trenches, so we replied with two heavy bombs. The first was a kind & the second burst in the air, impossible to tell whether effective or not. As the enemy stopped bombing, we did not continue to firing. At midday the infantry asked us to fire at the opposite trenches, to heavy bombs were fired all bursting, & judging by the amount of timber that was blown in the air the damage was great. The enemy replied with three bombs. In the afternoon the enemy turned his artillery onto our trenches and also his mortars undercover of their artillery. We did not reply. One of their shells landed in a dug out stores doing some damage to our stores, both guns were put out of action. Our casualties were one shrapnel that were not put out of action. Our casualties were one killed. The same evening our billet was shelled & one man was wounded.	
	3.8.15		Continued making a new gun emplacement.	
	4.8.15		Third gun emplacement was completed.	
	5.8.15		Enemy in the afternoon opened fire with their mortars,	

Army Form C. 2118

WAR DIARY
or
INTELLIGENCE SUMMARY
(Erase heading not required.)

42nd T. H. Bat.

Place	Date	Hour	Summary of Events and Information	Remarks and references to Appendices
In the field	5.8.15		sending over thirty bombs into our trenches. We replied with sioc, all of which detonated. One of our guns was buried, though not damaged, & all the men's dugouts (4) were blown in, & much kit destroyed. We had one man wounded. Carried two beds of the extreme left & prepared two new positions in the night.	X
"	6.8.15		In the early morning the enemy fired about 6 bombs from their mortars into our position, causing little damage, as the trenches which they fired at had been blown in already. We were not allowed to fire. Took two guns to the extreme left, taking one away from the right (146th Bde area) & continued digging gun positions	
"	7.8.15		Completed two gun emplacements on the left (148th Bde area) & began a new emplacement in the 146th Bde area, in lieu of the one destroyed.	

17/8/15

Army Form C. 2118

WAR DIARY
or
INTELLIGENCE SUMMARY
(Erase heading not required.)

42nd T.M. Bat.

Place	Date	Hour	Summary of Events and Information	Remarks and references to Appendices
Sheet 22 NW B29 a 34	8.8.15		Completed gun positions in the 148th Bde area. At 6.30 pm opened fire, firing altogether 40 heavy & 6 light bombs. Most of the light bombs burst in the air, but all the heavy detonated, five of them being effective. The enemy replied with two artillery. Our casualties were one man wounded. During the night the guns were brought back, the beds being left in their positions.	
	9.8.15		At 6.30 pm enemy's mortars opened fire, we replied with 10 heavy & 8 light bombs. 5 of which were duds, 10 detonating in enemy trenches.	
	10.8.15		At 4.30 am, German sent two bombs over in a mist, we fired 4 heavy in reply. 3 of which detonated, parapet being damaged.	
	11.8.15		At 3.45 am the enemy's mortars opened fire altogether 6 bombs being fired. We replied with 10 heavy bombs, 9 of which detonated. At midday the hostile mortars were again active. We fired 7 heavy and 2 light bombs all of which detonated. The enemy's parapet was breached in two places.	
	12.8.15		Quiet day	
	13.8.15		Quiet day	
	14.8.15		Quiet day.	

WAR DIARY or INTELLIGENCE SUMMARY

Army Form C. 2118

T.M. XLIX
42nd H. Battery
43rd T.M.B.

Place	Date	Hour	Summary of Events and Information	Remarks and references to Appendices
D Coy Trenches	16/8/15		Sunday — Quiet.	
	16/8/15		Quiet.	
	17/8/15		At stand to we fired 5 rifle bombs as everything had been very quiet during working hours behind their front trench. No reply from enemy. At midday fired another 6 bombs, their damage reports. We shot 7 bombs over and 9 at 11. In the afternoon Germans opened fire, we fired 3 heavy bombs, the end we saw they did little damage, enemy seeing fire discovered point of mineral. At 4 am double mortar opened fire, firing about 4 bombs Rapid and 9 light bombs at enemy trenches containing them, but nothing eventually opened fire of abstinent there nothing. Looks like a point out that we light bombs are not an effective reply to enemy bombs and any ammunition is absolutely inaccurate.	
	19/8/15		Quiet	
	20/8/15		Quiet	
	21/8/15		Quiet	

N Dennes
H. R.G.A.
Lt. H. Batty

Lt. H. R.G.A.
Lt. H. Batty
16/8/15

Army Form C. 2118

WAR DIARY
or
INTELLIGENCE SUMMARY

(Erase heading not required.)

42nd T.H. Battery

Place	Date	Hour	Summary of Events and Information	Remarks and references to Appendices
Breelen	22/8/15		Quiet day.	
	23/8/15		At 5.30 p.m. the enemy opened fire with their mortars. We replied with 5 light bombs all of which detonated. Our howitzers set a part of the enemy's trench on fire & two of our bombs burst at this spot.	
	24/8/15		Enemy's mortars became active at 7 p.m. firing about 5 bombs. We fired 10 light bombs four of which were blind. The damage done was considerable and timber was observed in the air.	
	25/8/15		We were relieved at 1.20 am by the 38th Battery, 6th Division & returned to the billet at Breelen.	
	26/8/15		Reconnoitred a new position at trench E 29.	
	27/8/15		Took working party up to trenches to prepare new positions.	
	28/8/15		Took over positions at E 29 from 37th Battery and also 2 beds and one gun.	

Army Form C. 2118

WAR DIARY
or
INTELLIGENCE SUMMARY
(Erase heading not required.)

T.M.42nd Front Line 4-7/7/15
XLIX

Place	Date	Hour	Summary of Events and Information	Remarks and references to Appendices
In the field	28/7/15		Left school at 6 p.m. & arrived at billets of trench howitzers of Division at 7.15.	
	29/7/15		Took over the front of 146th Inf. Bde. (T.F.). As there were 2 guns & 3 beds there already, I took them over from 37th Bat. & handed over same from 42nd Bat. to 37th Bat. Took up at night 1 gun & 18 heavy bombs, & detatchments for 3 guns.	
	30/7/15		Spent day making dug outs for guns & stores.	
	31/7/15		At 10.15 a.m. the Germans opened fire with a trench mortar. They fired 3 bombs; I replied with four heavy bombs, all of which detonated, doing considerable material damage. This stopped their mortar, but their field guns opened fire & one shell landed in one of our dug outs, breaking two tool boxes & some of the contents. In the afternoon continued digging dug outs. Brought up stores from R.E.s in the evening.	

3/6/15

WAR DIARY or INTELLIGENCE SUMMARY

(Erase heading not required.)

Army Form C. 2118

42nd Trench How. Bty. L

Instructions regarding War Diaries and Intelligence Summaries are contained in F.S. Regs., Part II. and the Staff Manual respectively. Title Pages will be prepared in manuscript.

Place	Date	Hour	Summary of Events and Information	Remarks and references to Appendices
In the field	5/9/15		Trenches in a very bad state, owing to recent rains. Repaired dug-out & bomb stores.	
	6/9/15		Trenches still too bad to work in.	
	7/9/15		Began a gun position in E.28 (trench)	
	8/9/15		Completed position & dug out in E.28.	
	9/9/15		Fired 4 heavy bombs in reply to enemy's grenades, all of which detonated doing considerable damage. One landed where a working party was observed previously and a lot of timber was seen in the air. The enemy ceased bombing so we stopped firing.	
	10/9/15		Began new gun position well forward in the sap E.29	
	11/9/15		Quiet day.	

[signature] 20/9/15

WAR DIARY
or
INTELLIGENCE SUMMARY

Army Form C. 2118

Hons. J. M. G. J
42nd Howitzer Battery

(Erase heading not required.)

Instructions regarding War Diaries and Intelligence Summaries are contained in F.S. Regs., Part II. and the Staff Manual respectively. Title Pages will be prepared in manuscript.

Place	Date	Hour	Summary of Events and Information	Remarks and references to Appendices
	12.9.15		Quiet day. Situation unchanged	
	13.9.15		Quiet day. Situation unchanged	
	14.9.15		Quiet day. Situation unchanged	
	15.9.15		Quiet day. Situation unchanged	
	16.9.15		Commenced new gun positions on Sep 6.2.9. Building new Officers and servants dug out in front line.	
	17.9.15		Finished above gun position	
	18.9.15		At 4.45 P.M. enemy sent over four hird mortars which exploded close behind (heavy) all of which detonated in the earth without a considerable amount of debris was thrown up & the howitzer seemed to have been damaged in our flank.	

M. Donald
2nd Lieut R.F.A.
in comdg 42nd H? Battery

WAR DIARY or INTELLIGENCE SUMMARY

Army Form C. 2118

42nd Trench Mortar Battery.

Place	Date	Hour	Summary of Events and Information	Remarks and references to Appendices
In the Field	19/9/15		Quiet day.	
	20/9/15		Deepened trench in front of left hand gun.	
	21/9/15		Quiet day.	
	22/9/15		We made a new dug out for the left hand gun, which now is only kept in position in day time, and is removed at night to a dug out near about the Detachment sleeps.	
	23/9/15		Quiet day.	
	24/9/15		Connected observation station with centre gun by telephone.	
	25/9/15		Our Artillery began to bombard the trenches at 3.30 a.m. They began to reply with their Artillery and Machine Gun and one heavy and one light were in return. We fired 5 light bombs and 6 light bombs in return. Also one heavy and one light were flints. Observation was a difficulty owing to the German trenches being covered with smoke, but 3 heavy burst in the German trench and seemed to do considerable damage. It is not possible to observe the result of the light bombs. Our casualties were nil but one of our Dug Outs was blown in.	

(Lt.) E.T. Kennedy R.G.A.
Commanding 42nd T.M. Battery

Army Form C. 2118

WAR DIARY
or
INTELLIGENCE SUMMARY   42 Trench Mortar Battery

(Erase heading not required.)

Instructions regarding War Diaries and Intelligence Summaries are contained in F. S. Regs., Part II. and the Staff Manual respectively. Title Pages will be prepared in manuscript.

Place	Date	Hour	Summary of Events and Information	Remarks and references to Appendices
In the field	26/9/15		Quiet. - Repairing dugout which was partly blown in during yesterdays bombardment.	
	27/9/15		Heavy rain, work impossible.	
	28/9/15		Heavily shelled, no recent bombers. We fired 4 light bombs from Right Hand Gun of which two were premature and 1 dud.	
	29/9/15		Repaired telephone wires. Quiet day.	
	30/9/15		Training & taking out trenches.	
	1/10/15		Cleaning out shewed reserve forward gun.	
	2/10/15		Laying trench guides.	

M Devonald
for O.C. 42 T.M.B.

5/10/15

WAR DIARY
INTELLIGENCE SUMMARY 4 2 T. M. Battery
(Erase heading not required.)

Army Form C. 2118

Place	Date	Hour	Summary of Events and Information	Remarks and references to Appendices
In the field	3/10/15		Trenches flooded out by heavy rain & work impossible.	
	4/10/15		Bailing out trenches and cleaning up positions.	
	5/10/15		Heavy mortaring to right of position and Colonel Infantry in E99 asked us to have fire 2 bombs into new enemy trench to 3.7 Battery. This was done. But 3 heavy.	
	6/10/15		Cleared trench which had partly fallen in near No. 2. Dug out first trench found in front of No. 3 Gun.	
	7/10/15		Cleared passage the No 3 gun which infantry had blocked up while deepening adjoining trench	
	8/10/15		Built Parados round No 1 gun & improved position generally.	
	9/10/15		Commenced taking up duck guides & re-laying near No 1 gun.	

10 December MPJG
2nd Lieut T.M.B.

WAR DIARY
or
INTELLIGENCE SUMMARY

42nd Battery

Army Form C. 2118

(Erase heading not required.)

Place	Date	Hour	Summary of Events and Information	Remarks and references to Appendices
	10/10/15.		Built up parados near left-hand gun, slot for right-hand gun	
	11/10/15.		Improved trench leading from left hand gun to main communication trench, fitted trench ghilas.	
	12/10/15.		Repaired telephone wires between middle + right-gun + head quarters. Also tested instruments. At-right began again & left gun also began to dig dug-out down in on the right of the ''. Infantry started to dig trench from left gun to Eclive Valley, making communication between left & centre gun much easier.	
	13/10/15.		Enemy may began a dug-out near centre gun. At two o'clock enemy commenced a strafe in cooperation with the artillery. Fired 3 rounds from left-gun which was then changing Gel's taken to my dugout, + all fell in a very near the booke Simultaneously the centre gun opened fire in the gap. Heavies then two light bombs then another hour heavies. All heavies did good execution + 1 light bomb was a dud. The right gun altogether fired 9 rounds (light) 6 of the 9 failed to explode, safety pins were withdrawn + defective points. Gun's infuse. Left hand gun emplacement much damaged by mortars + hand bombs. A new emplacement will have to be found. During the	

1875 Wt. W503/826 1,000,000 4/15 J.B.C. & A. A.D.S.S./Forms/C. 2118.

WAR DIARY or INTELLIGENCE SUMMARY

(Erase heading not required.)

Army Form C. 2118

Place: 42 Battery

Date	Hour	Summary of Events and Information	Remarks and references to Appendices
14/10/15		right we repaired damage done to dugouts & gun emplacements. Cut away left hand side of right gun emplacement to allow of a straighter rule on dugout. Carried on repair of left had dugout & night & during the day to filled sandbags for middle gun dugout.	
15/10/15		Continued on new position to left & new gun emplacement damaged by the enemy on Wed. 13/10/15. It could not be used for firing from again. (This new position has since been below up Sat. 16/10/15) with middle gun	
16/10/15		No morning progress was made. At 1.15 p.m. the enemy commenced a violent bombardment along the whole line. About 5 minutes after commencement of bombardment. The middle gun dugout was destroyed by a 5" howitzer shell & at this gun could not be used. This left me with only the right gun with which a steady fire was kept up till ammunition ran out. The average then came down the line than the Germans were	

WAR DIARY
or
INTELLIGENCE SUMMARY

Army Form C. 2118

Place: 42nd Battery

Date	Hour	Summary of Events and Information	Remarks and references to Appendices
16/10/15 (contd)		Coming over the parapet - we have no sure bombs left. I sent Hy [Heavy] guns back down s/pipe line kind where when the message returned to proved the nature I had of the guns brought back & went to dig out some more ammunition from the blown in bomb store. (It was impossible to do this before now to the many fire) & this enabled me to fire two more lights (fuses) & 4 of the sight gun fired 9 rounds & 6 charges & 5" tubes. Late in the evening we were short of these fixed blinds. I sent down to Brielen for more ammunition 5 more heavy bombs & 5" tubes & 6 charges & sent down to Bombardment La Bois for 4½ hours & there were no casualties among the battery. G.S. John-Smith 7/1/15	29/10/15

WAR DIARY
or
INTELLIGENCE SUMMARY
(Erase heading not required.)

Army Form C. 2118.

42nd Battery.
Trench Mortars.

Place	Date	Hour	Summary of Events and Information	Remarks and references to Appendices
	17/10/15		Repaired damage to emplacements & dugouts sustained in previous days bombardment; at night commenced new bomb store for centre gun.	
	18/10/15		Continued repair of bomb store (centre gun) took in telephone from gun in E.29 to observation station in sap head. Parapet & parados by night gun knocked in, commenced to rebuild same by night.	
	19/10/15		Fired 5 heavy bombs in reply to enemy at stand to in the morning, only one exploded, that in enemy sap. We were heavily shelled in the afternoon at 3 p.m, the right gun being buried but undamaged & the gunners dugout being blown in. Repaired same during the night.	
	20/10/15		Filled sandbags for dugout blown in yesterday (19") started rebuilding same after stand down at night. During day removed bed from left gun emplacement as this position was no longer tenable.	
	21/10/15		Took over 2 guns & beds from 28" Battery at Turco Farm K28/a	

1875 Wt. W593/826 1,000,000 4/15 J.B.C. & A. A.D.S.S./Forms/C. 2118.

WAR DIARY
or
INTELLIGENCE SUMMARY
(Erase heading not required.)

Army Form C. 2118

42 Battery
French Mortars

Place	Date	Hour	Summary of Events and Information	Remarks and references to Appendices
	22/10/15		Our trenches at Turco Farm were heavily shelled all day & officers dugout was blown in, one man wounded. By night commenced to rebuild officers dugout.	
	23/10/15		Continued with rebuilding of dugout - blown in yesterday.	

G. St John Smith
2" Lieut
for O.C. 42nd Battery.

WAR DIARY
or
INTELLIGENCE SUMMARY
(Erase heading not required.)

42nd T.M. Bat'y

Army Form C. 2118

Place	Date	Hour	Summary of Events and Information	Remarks and references to Appendices
In the field	23/10/15		The 37th Battery relieved us at Turco Farm and the 34th at E29. We brought one gun & bed complete from E29 to billet.	
	24/10/15		A motor lorry arrived at the billet with the 48th battery to which the infantry personnel of the 42nd battery were transferred. The 42nd battery then proceeded to Bailleul where the night was spent in billets.	
	25/10/15		The battery proceeded to Armentières and was billeted near the Pont-de-Nieppe.	
	26/10/15		The trenches 67-73 were allotted to the 42nd battery, which was changed into a composite battery, of 2 ? 1½" mortars, 1 ? 4" mortar and 1 4lb mortar. Suitable positions for these were reconnoitred in a general way.	
	27/10/15		The trenches 67-73 were carefully reconnoitred and positions chosen for gun positions, spare beds, dug outs etc.	
	28/10/15		2 out working parties consisting of four men each went to the trenches & began working. One party commenced dug out & gun position in trench 68 & Two parties worked in trench 70, at dug out and two gun positions. The fourth party began officers dug out in Lothian Avenue.	
	29/10/15		Above work continued. Men's billets were changed from Pont de Nieppe to Armentières.	2/11/15

Army Form C. 2118

WAR DIARY
or
INTELLIGENCE SUMMARY

(Erase heading not required.)

42nd T.M. Bat. Y

Place	Date	Hour	Summary of Events and Information	Remarks and references to Appendices
~~Fulhelm~~	31/10/15		The rain which lasted all day greatly interfered with work. The forward positions in trench 70 were full of water. Continued dig out in close support trench 70.	
I.10.C.9.3	1/11/15		Rained all day again. Positions in trench 70 completely flooded. Dug out near Haystack ram full of water. Commenced new dug out (officers) near Lothian Avenue + continued working on dug out in trench 70.	
	2/11/15		Dug out in Trench 67 nearly completed. Placed temporary roof on it. Raised old site for officers dug out to be the site of main bomb store for mortars in ylst sector (trenches 67 - 73)	
	3/11/15		Rain again interfered with work. Spent most of the day carrying timber + bricks to main bomb store. In evening brought timber + girders for officers dug out to trenches.	
	4/11/15		Began making framework for officers dug out + dug out channels for draining same. Placed trench boards in trench leading to officers dug out. In the evening brought down framework + roofing for bomb store.	

1875. Wt. W593/826 1,000,000 4/15 J.B.C. & A. A.D.S.S./Forms/C.2118.

Army Form C. 2118

WAR DIARY
or
INTELLIGENCE SUMMARY   42nd T.M. Bat^y
(Erase heading not required.)

Place	Date	Hour	Summary of Events and Information	Remarks and references to Appendices
In the field	5/11/15		Continued work on officers dug out, drainers & began erecting bomb store. Brought a lot of timber from dump to trenches	
I.10.c.9.3	6/11/15		Carried on work on bomb store & finished dug out in trench 67.	

G S John Swift Lt T.M.b.
(I/c O.C. 42nd T.M.b.)

WAR DIARY
or
INTELLIGENCE SUMMARY
(Erase heading not required.)

42nd T.M. Bat-y

Army Form C. 2118

Place	Date	Hour	Summary of Events and Information	Remarks and references to Appendices
Reference Sheet 2 36. N.W. C 25. c 3. 2.	7/11/15		Carried on work in gun position, trench 67. Brought up timber, chiefly 'sleepers' in evening	
	8/11/15		Completed bomb store, Completely boarding the floor & walls, laid bricks in front of it. Completed officers dug out	
	9/11/15		Put up frame work of servant's dug out. Found that all gun positions in 67 & 70 were ~~---~~ too damp owing to the room, so carried up sleepers and bricks to positions to make them firm. Completed servant's dug out. Made dug out in 67 into a subsidiary bomb store & commenced a new dug out in its place, carried up timber to 67. Brought up to bombstore in evening one ('four inch') & one (4 pounder) mortar & bombs for same.	
	10/4/15		Continued work on men's dug out's in 67 & 70 & on bombstore in 67. Carried bombs from battalion bomb store to bomb store in Lothian Avenue (4 pounder bombs). Brought	
	11/11/15		bombs (1½") to bomb store from billets	

Army Form C. 2118

WAR DIARY
or
INTELLIGENCE SUMMARY
(Erase heading not required.)

42nd Trench Mortar Battery

Place	Date	Hour	Summary of Events and Information	Remarks and references to Appendices
Reference Sheet 2. 36.N.W. C.25.c.3.2	12/4/15		Poured all day. Little work done. Spent most of the day carrying sleepers & bricks from Dump to trenches 67 & 7.	
	13/4/15		Poured again all day. Trenches in a very bad state. After Cleared trench in front of gun position in 67, where the parapet had fallen. Gun position on left of trench 70 full of water. Commenced new position.	

T.C.Kennedy
2/Lt R.F.A.
O.C. 42nd T.M.Bat.y

WAR DIARY or INTELLIGENCE SUMMARY

Army Form C. 2118

42nd T.M.Bat.

Place	Date	Hour	Summary of Events and Information	Remarks and references to Appendices
36 N.W. Sheet 2 C 25.c.3.9	14/4/15.		Continued work in strengthening bomb store (subsidiary) in trench 67. In evening brought heavy bombs (2" mortar) gun to main bomb store. Placed bed in trench 70 & raised parapet protecting position from enfilade fire.	
	15/4/15.		Bomb store was found to be too congested & rearranged bombs. Kept the 2" mortar beds outside. Continued work on subsidiary bomb store in 67 & gun position in 70.	
	16/4/15.		Brought one 1½" mortar & bombs & 3.7" mortar to trench 70. In the afternoon fired 6 heavy & 3 light bombs & 10 jam-tin bombs at trenches opposite 70. The 1½ mortar bombs all failed to detonate except 1 heavy bomb, which fell short & burst in the water in narrow lit. The jam tins were more successful, all bursting, most of them in the enemy's trenches. The enemy replied with field guns & mortars of the "sausage" class but did little damage.	
	17/4/15.		Detachments went into trenches, 4 men in 70 & 4 in 67. Completed dugouts in above trenches & bomb store in 67. Carried bricks to dugouts after dark.	
	18/4/15.		Began new gun position on the nightof trench 70 in disused trench in front of close support trench. Deepened this trench & building barricade in front of gun position.	

Army Form C. 2118

WAR DIARY
or
INTELLIGENCE SUMMARY
(Erase heading not required.)

42nd T.M. Bat

Place	Date	Hour	Summary of Events and Information	Remarks and references to Appendices
36 N.W. Sheet 2 C.25.C.2.2.	18/4/15		Carried sleepers to gun position.	
	19/4/15		The infantry had drained their trenches into the ground in front of gun position left in right of trench 70. Laid trench boards over the water & continued gun position on right of trench, making small bomb-stores, observation, dugout	
	20/4/15		Added overhead cover to gun position at left of 70. At 3h.pm fired 4 heavy bombs from left of 70, 6 light bombs from right & 10 am-tins. The 1½" mortar bombs were fuzed as follows:— light bombs; new fuzes which had been kept perfectly dry. Heavy bombs, 3 old fuzes which had suffered from damp & 1 new fuze with springs taken out of fuze. All these fuzes had been kept wrapped up in cotton wool before a fire for two days previous. The Heavy bombs were unsuccessful only the one fuzed with new fuze bursting. This did some damage to enemy's wire. The light bombs were more successful, only 2 failing to burst. The last two fired both landed on a hard dugout probably concrete as sparks arose when they landed. They both detonated but it was impossible to see the damage done as it was getting dark. The T.M.	

WAR DIARY
or
INTELLIGENCE SUMMARY
(Erase heading not required.)

42ⁿᵈ T.M. Bat.

Army Form C. 2118

Place	Date	Hour	Summary of Events and Information	Remarks and references to Appendices
36 N.W. Sheet 8. C.25.c.3.2	20/11/15		Jam tin bombs were very successful all detonating in "or" just behind the enemy's trenches. The enemy replied with mortars, field guns & machine guns, the latter causing most annoyance though no damage was done. (sd) T.C. Kennedy. 2/Lt. R.F.A. O.C. 42ⁿᵈ T.M. 13	

WAR DIARY
or
INTELLIGENCE SUMMARY

Army Form C. 2118.

2nd Trench Mortar Battery

Place	Date	Hour	Summary of Events and Information	Remarks and references to Appendices
10.B.5.5.	21/11/15	8.30 am	Commenced new emplacement in trench 67 to a	
		3pm	2" gun. Jolly sandbags & cotty out was all that could	36
			be done by day.	
10.B.5.5.		5.30pm to 7.30pm	Put up parapet round emplacement & overcoat with sacks to prevent it being seen from the enemy lines.	
11.C.3.5.	22/11/15	8.30am to 12.30	Finis bed overhead cover for position on left of minniwerfer in trench 70. Made bomb store for right trench gun in minniwerfer.	Log sheet
10.B.5.5.		2 - 4.30 pm	Continued building position (2") in trench 67.	
10.B.5.5.	23/11/15	8.30 12.30	Sandbagged & put bricks on roof of dugout in 70 trench. Fetched 22 sleepers from Haystack Farm for 2" bed in 67 & for overhead cover for gun.	Reference No 1

Army Form C. 2118.

2nd Trench
42' Mortar Battery

WAR DIARY
or
INTELLIGENCE SUMMARY.
(Erase heading not required.)

Place	Date	Hour	Summary of Events and Information	Remarks and references to Appendices
10.B.5.6		2.30p- 6.4-3.p.	Rearranged bomb store near officers dugout & cases for all ammunition.	
10.B.5.5		5.30 pm -7.30	Improved parapet in 67 for 2" gun.	
10.B.5.5.	24/11/15	8.30 6.12-30	Fired 2" position in 67 with sandbags to enable 4" R.M.L. gun to be fired in the afternoon.	
		3 pm	Fired 9 rounds from 4" gun at 300 yds. The first round fell short, but the remaining 8 exploded well in & near the hostile front line trench opposite 67. No blinds. As the gun round the rifle mechanism jammed & we could fire no more ammn. for the time being.	
10.B.5.5"	25/11/15	8.30 am	Commenced putty in wooden frame in 67 trench 2	
		12.3.00	Emplacement, first removed sandbag lining which was only a temporary revetment.	

Army Form C. 2118.

WAR DIARY
or
INTELLIGENCE SUMMARY.
(Erase heading not required.)

42nd 7.17.13.

Instructions regarding War Diaries and Intelligence Summaries are contained in F.S. Regs., Part II. and the Staff Manual respectively. Title pages will be prepared in manuscript.

Place	Date	Hour	Summary of Events and Information	Remarks and references to Appendices
10.B.5.6.	25/11/15	2-4pm	Continued on 2" position in trench 67.	
10.B.5.5.	26/11/15	9:30am to 12:30am	Carried War siders to 2" position in 67 for overhead cover for the gun. Laid sleepers to ready lid on.	
		2-4pm	Continued with work on this emplacement.	
10.B.5.5.	27/11/15	8-30 to 12:30	Fetched corrugated iron sheets & cut them to size for novelty roof of emplacement.	
		2-4pm	Picked space between with sandbags.	

G.S. John Smith
O.C. 42nd Trench Mortar Battery.

WAR DIARY
or
INTELLIGENCE SUMMARY.   42nd T.M. Battery

Army Form C. 2118.

Place	Date	Hour	Summary of Events and Information	Remarks and references to Appendices
11 Div	Nov 29		making emplacements.	8/1/Y
	30		do —	
	Dec 1st		Fired two 50lb bombs into Trench WEZ MACQUART. Detonations good.	
	2nd		do. Fired two light 15"— 1 kind } Int. trench opposite one heavy. — good } Mushroom	
	3rd		do. " two light 15" — 1 kind } — do 1 good }	
	4th		do — do	
	5th		do. Fired two big W 15" — good. — do	

E.T.Baird

A Abibison Lt
Comdg 42 Bty T. Mortars

WAR DIARY or INTELLIGENCE SUMMARY

Army Form C. 2118

1/X/15/1

42 T.M. Bty. R.G.A.

Place	Date	Hour	Summary of Events and Information	Remarks and references to Appendices
2.1 Div	1915 Dec. 6th		III Building emplacement — Fired at Trench opposite WILSH ROOM" 2" = 2 ; 1½"(l) = 2 ; 4lb = 4 = all good	
"	7th		— do — Fired at E Trench opposite 67 2" = 2 (good, 1 know); 1½"(h) = 1 good, 1½"(l) = 4 (2 good, 2 blind) 4lb = 4 (3 good, 1 blind)	
"	8th		≡ Enemy retaliated with 5.9 shell. ≡ Building emplacements. Fired at points 50 opposite Trench 67 = 2" = 14 good blind 1½"(h) = 10 10 4 1½"(l) = 14 8 2 4lb = 20 6 8 20 Nil Enemy retaliated with 5.9" shell. Whizz bangs and Rifle Grenades. Pte Carnes. J. No 15000, 10 Yorks Reg. attd 134 who killed by a shell after our firing was finished.	
"	9 10 11 12		⌐ Building emplacement	

W Hobson 2nd Lieut
Comg 42 T.M. Bty

Page 1 of — H.2nd TRENCH MORTAR BATTERY

WAR DIARY
INTELLIGENCE SUMMARY

Army Form C. 2118

Place	Date 1915	Hour	Summary of Events and Information	Remarks and references to Appendices
21st Division Trenches B4 B5 43	Dec 12th & 13th		Work on Emplacements & Bomb Stores	
	15th		Fired five Ranging Shots	
	16th	14.30	In co-operation with Artillery, the Trench mortars took being to block trenches on either flank subjected to night-assault. Fired 53 Rounds. All detonated properly. Our mortar positions in Trenches 69, 40, 41, & 42. The German Artillery quickly located our positions & heavily shelled us. One Corporal was slightly wounded & two mortars slightly damaged	
	17th to 19th		Work on emplacements & Bomb Stores	
	20th		Fired in retaliation 17 Bombs about 10 P.M.; 2 – 50 lb Bombs	
	21st		Fired 4 Ranging Shots	
	22nd		Co-operated with Artillery, firing in Trenches opposite 40 and 41. Fired 64 Rounds all detonated well. Received heavy retaliation, 2 mortars slightly damaged	
	23rd		Fired 2 rounds in retaliation to Bombs	

WAR DIARY or INTELLIGENCE SUMMARY

42nd TRENCH MORTAR BATTERY

Place	Date	Hour	Summary of Events and Information	Remarks and references to Appendices
21st Division Trenches O1 b 6.4 to 4.3	1915 Dec 2nd & 3rd to 24th		Work on emplacements & Bomb Stores. Co-operated with Artillery firing on trenches 40 & 41, fired 40 rounds. All detonated well. Received heavy retaliation. Two mortars slightly damaged. One man severely wounded. Wind militated against accurate firing.	
	25th to 31st		Work on emplacements, Bomb stores, etc.	

A. Wilson 2L. RFA.
Comdg 42 T.M. Battery
RGA

9. & 2 Trench Mortar Bty
Jan
Vol VII

Part I

42ⁿᵈ Trench Mortar Bty

Army Form C. 2118.

WAR DIARY
or
INTELLIGENCE SUMMARY.
(Erase heading not required.)

42ⁿᵈ Trench Mortar Battery

Instructions regarding War Diaries and Intelligence Summaries are contained in F. S. Regs., Part II. and the Staff Manual respectively. Title pages will be prepared in manuscript.

Place	Date	Hour	Summary of Events and Information	Remarks and references to Appendices
Ioda 2	1/1/16		General work on emplacements.	
	2/1/16		Selected position for permanent reserve emplacement, 2" Gun.	
	3/1/16		Fired 4–3.3lb bombs at enemy seen opposite Trench 70 with poor effect.	
	4/1/16		Fired 9–3.3lb bombs at enemy seen opposite Trench 70 from first emplacement. Fired 4–3.3lb bombs (1 dud) at enemy opposite Trench 70, distance accurate.	
	5/1/16		Started permanent reserve emplacement in centre for 2" gun.	
	6/1/16		Work on permanent reserve emplacement 2" Gun in centre.	
	6/1/16		General work on emplacements. Also on permanent reserve emplacement.	
	7/1/16		Preparation of two positions for bombardment 8/1/16.	
			Carried ammunition from billet to emplacement in Trench 70.	
	8/1/16		Completed work for bombardment. Fired 15. 60lb Bombs. 25. 7lb Bombs at enemy seen opposite Trench 70.	
			Clearing up guns and emplacements.	
	9/1/16		General work on emplacements.	

Page 11

Army Form C. 2118.

WAR DIARY
or
INTELLIGENCE SUMMARY.
(Erase heading not required.)

Place	Date	Hour	Summary of Events and Information	Remarks and references to Appendices
Liod 1.2	10/1/16		Preparation for bombardment for 11/1/16. Carne received ammunition for bombardment. Fired 25 3.16 Bombs, 21-60 lb Bombs at Crater Ellwood. Front 70, also 4L, 4.6 Bombs at enemy trench. Very satisfactory enemy trench at range.	
	11/1/16		Continued to attend to permanent record emplacement going to water, commenced new one me top.	
	12/1/16		Worked on Permanent Reserve Emplacement, dug out for men & Bomb Store.	
	13/1/16		General work on emplacement, bomb store. Continues Reserve Emplacement as a unit.	
	14/1/16		Work on Permanent Reserve Emplacement in Crater.	
	15/1/16		Work on Permanent Reserve Emplacement. Dug-out finished. General work on emplacement. Carried 13" gun & two beds back	
	16/1/16		to billets for run to another battery.	
	17/1/16		Released Bomb Store in Trench 67, damage by enemy fire	

Army Form C. 2118.

WAR DIARY
or
INTELLIGENCE SUMMARY.
(Erase heading not required.)

Page 1

Place	Date	Hour	Summary of Events and Information	Remarks and references to Appendices
Trod	1-2/9/16		Continue work on Reserve Emplacement in Centre & the relief & parties for new emplacement on right.	
	20/9/16		Fired 5. 6.0lb Bombs at three at way marked.	
	21/9/16		Work on Recon Emplacement.	
			Fired 8. 6.0lb Bombs at those at way marked. Enemy retaliates heavily, many rounds missing 2" mortar in 67.	
	22/9/16		Preparation for bombardment to 24/9/16 & 25/9/16.	
			Commenced new 1" Gun emplacement in Trench 69.	
	23/9/16		Continue work on new 2" emplacement in Trench 69.	
			Made 1½" Gun emplacement in Trench 70.	
	24/9/16		Carry Bombs up for bombardment.	
			Fired 30. 3¾lb Bombs.	
			10. 6.0lb Bombs. (Emplacement became centrals).	
			Enemy action attempts to gun emplacement in Trench 69.	
	25/9/16		Improve 2" Gun emplacement in 69, & erects cover for other emplacement.	

T2134. Wt. W708—776. 500000. 4/15. Sir J. C. & S.

WAR DIARY
or
INTELLIGENCE SUMMARY.
(Erase heading not required.)

Army Form C. 2118.

Part IV

Place	Date	Hour	Summary of Events and Information	Remarks and references to Appendices
	25/1/16		Fired at Aeroplane (Night bombardment) in trench bombardment. Fired on aircraft.	
			F. 60.16 Rounds	
			15. 33.16 Rounds	
			6. 9.16 Rounds (Rifles, rifle mechanisms (two) cases cleaned)	
	26/1/16		Remover all guns to Main Road. Stop cellar Baty firing in trench 70. Returns employments.	
	27/1/16		Continued work on Permanent Reserve Emplacements in centre, also on Right working all night on hutts.	
	28/1/16		Continued General work on Reserve Emplacements, ratli enemy heavily bombarder whole sector in afternoon.	
	29/1/16		General work in 'Spencers' Chancel 2" gun emplacement in Trench 67 outgrown by enemy, trenches bed.	
	30/1/16		Work on Permanent Reserve Emplacement on Right, Camouflage from Pence tomb store in Trench 71 support to Central loop. General work in 'Spencers' retained. Wounded handed to 2"G emplacement in Trench 69. damaged by enemy shells. Wire work on Reserve Emplacement on Right.	
	31/1/16			
				S. Apr[?] 2nd Lt.
				O.C. 72 Engineers [?]

T2134. Wt. W708—776. 500000. 4/15. Sir J. C. & S.

Army Form C. 2118.

WAR DIARY
or
INTELLIGENCE SUMMARY.

(Erase heading not required.)

2ⁿᵈ Trench Mortar School
for February 1916

Vol. VIII

Place	Date	Hour	Summary of Events and Information	Remarks and references to Appendices
Solesmes	1/2/16			
	2/2/16			
	3/2/16			
	4/2/16			
	5/2/16		General work on Emplacements, Entrenching on	
	6/2/16		Permanent Reserve Emplacements.	
	7/2/16		Clearing up work in Bomb Store etc.	
	8/2/16			
	9/2/16			
	10/2/16			
	11/2/16			
	12/2/16			
	13/2/16			
	14/2/16			
	15/2/16			
	16/2/16			

WAR DIARY
or
INTELLIGENCE SUMMARY.
(Erase heading not required.)

Army Form C. 2118.

18/3/13

February 1916 (Coy)

Place	Date	Hour	Summary of Events and Information	Remarks and references to Appendices
Sofa 25	17/2/16			
	18/2/16		General work – Preparation of Position, and	
	19/2/16		Construction of work on Permanent Reserve	
	20/2/16		Emplacements.	
	21/2/16			
	22/2/16			
	23/2/16			
	24/2/16		Since 31. 1800 Bombs at Enemy trench assisting	
			Infantry in Night Bombing Raid. Enemy very poor,	
			a raid put about 15 yards long made in enemy front lines.	
	25/2/16			
	26/2/16		General work in trenches.	
	27/2/16			Japan, ft
	28/2/16			Ft. 9.2 Fortburton
	29/2/16			
			N.B. An exceedingly quiet month. No Offensive Ops, & a	
			mild enough month by Infantry, importing, Engineers, Artillery,	
			Company - everywhere Infantry takes far immunity from	
			Shelling, to enemy wished to complete.	

: **WAR DIARY**

or

INTELLIGENCE SUMMARY

Army Form C. 2118

4th XIV

Vol 172

421 T. Howitzer Battery
March 1916.
S.B. Slater y/hr
O.C. 421 T.H. Batty.

Army Form C. 2118.

WAR DIARY
or
INTELLIGENCE SUMMARY
(Erase heading not required.)

Instructions regarding War Diaries and Intelligence Summaries are contained in F. S. Regs., Part II. and the Staff Manual respectively. Title Pages will be prepared in manuscript.

Place	Date	Hour	Summary of Events and Information	Remarks and references to Appendices
SIMENCOURT	2.3.16		Battery went to 3rd Army Trench Mortar School at VALHEUREUX to draw four 3.7 inch trench howitzers, and undergo instruction in use of same.	
ARRAS	9.3.16		Battery returned to ARRAS and took up billets there. The need for Trench Mortar was not immediately felt and accordingly though positions, dug-outs, & bomb stores were chosen, battery did not go into action.	
	24.3.16		Officer steam took three guns into section held by 42nd Inf. Bde and same night ammunition for same was sent-up. One gun was placed in position.	
	25.3.16		Four bombs were fired from gun already placed (No 4 gun position:- Dur map 51/3. M4, B.5, 8. This gun is fired into enemy lines between points M4, B7,1, & M4 B10,1½. 9 shots were effective rifle exploded. The 9th Rifle Brigade were in right section of 42nd Inf. Bde front 9 5th Ox. AND BUCKS in the left sector.	
	26.3.16		The position of the three remaining guns is as follows (map as above) No 3 gun point M4, B.2, 3, fires in direction German lines between points M4, D.6,10 & M4, D6,6. No 2 gun is at M10, A 8,9 fires S.E towards M10, B.3½,7. No 1 gun is at M10, B1,4, and fires S.E towards M10, B.5, 8. In retaliation for German rifle-grenades, No 3 gun & No 4 gun fired four rounds each, (No 4 gun) burst very effectively a few feet above enemy parapet.	

EBStile 9W
42/1 T.H. Batty.

Army Form C. 2118.

WAR DIARY
or
INTELLIGENCE SUMMARY

(Erase heading not required.)

Instructions regarding War Diaries and Intelligence Summaries are contained in F. S. Regs., Part II. and the Staff Manual respectively. Title Pages will be prepared in manuscript.

Place	Date	Hour	Summary of Events and Information	Remarks and references to Appendices
ARRAS.	27.3.16		Two rounds were fired from No 4 gun in response to German rifle grenades. The battery was instructed to reply grenade, shell for grenade, with one round for each rifle grenade, & one round for each mortar. The personnel is becoming experienced in using fuze shorter than the given range of fuze later.	
	28.3.16		Two bombs were fired by No 1 gun, and burst just above enemy parapet, this is most effective as obtained by slightly shortening the given fuze length. The enemy put over two catapult bombs to which we replied.	
	29.3.16		The Stokes' battery not have been formed as yet, the light but four pounder bombs have towards a means of retaliation for enemy light Minenwerfer shells which are of course heavier. We gave as near as possible two for one. No 3 gun fired 9 rounds & No 1 3 rounds. Infantry Battalion relief accomplished without incident. The need for trench mortars behind the left of the left battalion is not yet felt, & ground is so flat that concealment of position would be difficult.	
	30.3.16	About 3.30 P.M.	enemy threw several rifle grenades into H 32, & on No 3 gun fired 6 rounds into enemy line between points M4, D.6, 10 & M4, D.6, 6. —	
	31.3.16		No 1 gun fired two rounds. The day was quiet except through a few rifle grenades were sent over H 32. Though some misunderstanding these were not energetically replied to by the mortars, though Infantry 9th KRRC replied with rifle grenades.	Sd E Elden? 2/Lt

Army Form C. 2118.

WAR DIARY
or
INTELLIGENCE SUMMARY

(Erase heading not required.)

Instructions regarding War Diaries and Intelligence Summaries are contained in F. S. Regs., Part II. and the Staff Manual respectively. Title Pages will be prepared in manuscript.

Place	Date	Hour	Summary of Events and Information	Remarks and references to Appendices

2449 Wt. W14957/M90 750,000 1/16 J.B.C. & A. Forms/C.2118/12.

Army Form C. 2118.

WAR DIARY
or
INTELLIGENCE SUMMARY

(Erase heading not required.)

Instructions regarding War Diaries and Intelligence Summaries are contained in F. S. Regs., Part II. and the Staff Manual respectively. Title Pages will be prepared in manuscript.

Place	Date	Hour	Summary of Events and Information	Remarks and references to Appendices
ARRAS	1-4-16		No 1 gun & No 2 gun Each fired two rounds in retaliation for rifle grenades. Prompt retaliation has very excellent effect on the enemy. Sentries are placed by the battery & it is their duty to reply without orders to any enemy mortar or grenade activity. No 3 gun fired 16 rounds, four of which failed to explode though excellent results were obtained from others. No 1 gun was out of action due to defective mechanism. This is being repaired.	
	2.4.16		Enemy active in morning and afternoon on left sector of Right battalion front. Rifle grenades, small Minenwerfer bombs, & heavy (ditto) were sent over. We replied energetically. No 2 gun fired ten rounds, & No 4 twenty rounds all of which exploded effectively	
	3.4.16		Quiet morning. O.C. Ruf.t In visited gun positions expressed satisfaction. Rifle grenades were sent over about 2 P.M. No 4 gun fired 11 four rounds, while No 2 gun fired eighteen. Officers 9th KRRC A Coy report that work of this gun was very good.	
	4.4.16		Quiet almost all day. No 1 gun is again in action. A few rifle grenades were sent over by the enemy later in the evening. This gun nevertheless fired ten rounds, while No 2 gun supported with four rounds.	
	5.4.16		Nothing of importance occurred. One firing was done in R.B. 9 & 5 Ox. & B.k.i. are now in line Infantry battalion relief took place without incident.	S B Slatin M 47/1 T.M.Batty

Army Form C. 2118.

WAR DIARY
or
INTELLIGENCE SUMMARY
(Erase heading not required.)

Place	Date	Hour	Summary of Events and Information	Remarks and references to Appendices
ARRAS	6.4.16		Information comes that large supplies of 3.7 ammunition are available as this type of mortar is shortly to be replaced it is desired to fire off as much of this as possible. We are therefore firing three shells bombs as retaliation for one enemy projectile. Only two rounds were fired from No 2 gun.	
	7.4.16		About 6 pm enemy hit over several bombs at stand to, and we fired seven rounds from No 1 gun, three of which are believed to have fallen in enemy front line.	
	8.4.16		Twenty two rounds were fired in all during the day No 3 gun did not fire, but remainder were responsible for the firing.	
	9.4.16		Considerable activity on part of enemy: rifle grenades, various bombs & mortars were put over during the day, and we replied vigorously. All the guns fired in all sixty rounds only two failing to explode. Field officer of 9th Rifle Brigade observed many of our rounds & reported they burst very accurately above enemy parapet. As these four rounder bombs are shrapnel-filled they should be most effective.	
	10.4.16		We were again active, forty five rounds being fired. No 3 gun fired 15 rounds in direction M4, D 6, 6. No 1 gun fired 30 rounds towards M 10, B 5, 8. There was only one "blind" round.	

SBSlater 2/Lt

WAR DIARY
or
INTELLIGENCE SUMMARY

Army Form C. 2118.

Place	Date	Hour	Summary of Events and Information	Remarks and references to Appendices
ARRAS	11.4.16		A quiet day for us. Only ten rounds were fired in retaliation for a few enemy rifle grenades. No 4 fired all ten rounds about 3 P.M.	
			Staff Officer of VI Corps visited all mortar positions on the Brigade front, and expressed himself as very satisfied that positions were chosen with a view to avoiding adequate for man firing the mortar.	
	12.4.16		A very quiet day. No firing was done by us.	
	13.4.16		Actively on the night of our line, No 1 gun fired forty rounds with very good accuracy. No 3 gun fired five rounds, the fifth however was disastrous & a premature burst. The gun was blown in half & two men of the battery were wounded, one subsequently died. The cause was most probably defective luting of the front. Infantry relief took place without incident. 9th KRRC & 5th KSLI are now in the line.	
	14.4.16		Battery fired 28 rounds one of which failed to explode. No 1 gun was drawn from the right to take up position of No 3. (No 2 gun will be referred to in future for convenience sake as No 2 and not re-numbered No 1)	
	15.4.16		Twelve rounds were fired, 9 all exploded. No 2 gun fired nine rounds & No 4, 3 rounds. Work was done on all the positions to make them additionally secure for firing of the gun.	
				SR Blake 2/Lt

Army Form C. 2118.

WAR DIARY
or
INTELLIGENCE SUMMARY

(Erase heading not required.)

Instructions regarding War Diaries and Intelligence Summaries are contained in F. S. Regs, Part II and the Staff Manual respectively. Title Pages will be prepared in manuscript.

Place	Date	Hour	Summary of Events and Information	Remarks and references to Appendices
ARRAS	16.4.4.		No. 3 gun fired twenty rounds carefully traversing enemy frontline between M.4.D.6,10. TM.4.D.6.6. Enemy were firing rifles at aeroplane and it is hoped some were hit. We are informed Germans knock in their trenches to fire at aircraft. No 4 fired 13 rounds.	
	17.4.4		No activity on either side. Two rounds were fired by No 2 gun. Trench Mortar exploded. A very quiet day.	
	18.4.4.		Prompt retaliation has somewhat lessened enemy activity. We put over 5 rounds from No 4 gun. Work was done on gun positions. It was to make them inconspicuous to aircraft. A complicated strenuous scheme for emplacements is fatal, though frequently plans for such emplacements are put before us.	
	19.4.4		Two shots were fired by No 3 gun, but otherwise no firing was done by us.	
	20.4.4.		No firing was done. A very quiet day.	

E.J. Slater 2/Lt

Army Form C. 2118.

WAR DIARY
or
INTELLIGENCE SUMMARY
(Erase heading not required.)

Instructions regarding War Diaries and Intelligence Summaries are contained in F. S. Regs., Part II. and the Staff Manual respectively. Title Pages will be prepared in manuscript.

Place	Date	Hour	Summary of Events and Information	Remarks and references to Appendices
ARRAS	21.4.16		No 3 gun firing over H 34 at 280 yds range fired 5 rounds traversing enemy front line. Two shots at 300 yds range also point from which enemy arc. observed to fire rifle grenades. No 2 gun fired 10 at 240 yds hits Maison Goole (Pts. M 10, B 2½, 7) and from at 270 yds at enemy front-line. Total fired 21 rounds. Infantry relief took place 9th R.B. & 5th Ox. & B.L.I. are in the line.	
	22.4.16		No 3 gun fired 11 rounds at 280 yds. four fuses to explode. No 2 gun fired 5 rounds shot three as burst med.- way between enemy front line and ours, one 'blind' round. This trouble is attributed to defective detonators, has been duly reported.	
	23.4.16		No firing at all, guns were thoroughly cleaned & overhauled.	
	24.4.16		9 rounds from No 3 gun at german loopholes in front line. Four-pounder bombs do not do much damage to trench and accordingly later in the evening medium battery Y.114. & Stokes battery took on organized shoot on enemy loopholes.	
	25.4.16		Everything quiet. No rounds were fired, a day passed without incident.	

SBSextn 7/M

WAR DIARY
or
INTELLIGENCE SUMMARY

(Erase heading not required.)

Army Form C. 2118.

Place	Date	Hour	Summary of Events and Information	Remarks and references to Appendices
ARRAS	26.4.16		Twenty-one rounds fired by No 3 gun at varying ranges, two air bursts & one blind round. This occurred in morning. At night twenty rounds fired from same gun at German salient opposite H.34, of these two were air bursts, two duds. No 2 gun fired four effective rounds.	
	27.4.16		An organised shoot was arranged by O.C. 9th K.R.B on loopholes etc in German salient opposite H.34. 3·7 Co-operated with Y.14 medium T.M. Battery & 42/2 Stokes Battery. 3·7 fired 41 rounds only two of which were ineffective.	
	28.4.16		No 2 gun fired seven rounds, and all were effective	
	29.4.16		In retaliation for a rifle-grenade about 8 p.m. then No 2 gun fired one round 9th K.R.R.C & 5th K.S.L.I. came into the Brigade front	
	30.4.16		A very quiet day. No rounds fired by the battery	

C.B. Slade 2/Lt.
h/1. Trench Howitzer
Battery

Army Form C. 2118.

WAR DIARY
or
INTELLIGENCE SUMMARY

(Erase heading not required.)

Instructions regarding War Diaries and Intelligence Summaries are contained in F. S. Regs., Part II. and the Staff Manual respectively. Title Pages will be prepared in manuscript.

Place	Date	Hour	Summary of Events and Information	Remarks and references to Appendices
	28-4-16			

2449 Wt. W14957/M90 750,000 1/16 J.B.C. & A. Forms/C.2118/12.

WAR DIARY
or
INTELLIGENCE SUMMARY
(Erase heading not required.)

Army Form C. 2118.

XIV

42/2 T M Bty
March 16
Vol 1 + 2

Army Form C. 2118.

WAR DIARY
or
INTELLIGENCE SUMMARY

(Erase heading not required.)

Month of April

Instructions regarding War Diaries and Intelligence Summaries are contained in F. S. Regs., Part II. and the Staff Manual respectively. Title Pages will be prepared in manuscript.

Place	Date	Hour	Summary of Events and Information	Remarks and references to Appendices
Arras	6.4.16.		Battery went by bus from SIMENCOURT to LIGNY-ST-FLOCHEL to 3rd Army Trench Mortar School to receive instruction in use of same STOKES gun, and to receive instruction in use of same.	
	12-4-16.		Battery returned to billets in ARRAS bringing from STOKES guns.	
	13-4-16		Battery remained in ARRAS, & details of their kits were completed	
	14.4.16.		Positions in section held by 142ND INF. BDE chosen for two guns (14th Div.) TRENCH MAP 51B N.W.3. Position of No 1 gun. M10.A.9½,5'. Position of No 2 gun:- M4.D.1½,2,5. The battery was divided into teams and preparation made for taking two guns into action the following day.	
	15.4.16.		At 8-15 p.m. team took two guns into line, left section was held by 5th K.S.L.I. & right section of brigade front by 9th K.R.R.C. guns were dug in & partly took up an initial supply of ammunition, thirty-nine STOKES bombs	
	16.4.16		At 4.15 A.M. both guns were in action retaliating for light trench mortars, & rained bombs. The latter had become somewhat numerous during the previous week but no more than ten were put over on this occasion due to prompt retaliation from STOKES guns. No 1 gun fired nine bombs & No 2, six. The first shell fired from No 1 gun jammed a dud, but from which smoke was seen to issue. An attempt was made to locate rancel bomb thrower, but without success.	

Geo. G. Sharp
Lt. 4/1 L.M.B.

Army Form C. 2118.

WAR DIARY
or
INTELLIGENCE SUMMARY
(Erase heading not required.)

Instructions regarding War Diaries and Intelligence Summaries are contained in F. S. Regs., Part II. and the Staff Manual respectively. Title Pages will be prepared in manuscript.

Place	Date	Hour	Summary of Events and Information	Remarks and references to Appendices
ARRAS	17.4.16		It was thought advisable to place another Stokes gun in position between points (MAP REFERENCE. Trench Map 51.B.) M10 C 4,4, & M10, A 9½, 5. On examination dis lance from enemy lines was found to be great. The gun is greatly handicapped by the loss of 130 yds range due to the withdrawal of red cartridge. 40 rounds were fire from gun No 1 & No 2.	
	18.4.16		A very quiet day. No 2 gun fired four rounds, one of which failed to explode, and No 1 gun fired one	
	19.4.16		No rounds fired. Relief of teams accomplished without incident. 9th KRRC annihilated German patrol. One prisoner captured reported that in his company most of the casualties are caused by our Trench mortars which are dead listed.	
	20.4.16		The enemy again fired a few varied bombs, but was quickly engaged. No 1 gun fired one round, & No 2 put three rounds into enemy front line at points M 4, D 6, 6.	
	21.4.16		Stokes' gun retaliated for light minenwerfer bombs but experienced difficulty in locating the enemy mortar which was firing. No 1 fired 11 rounds. At maximum range into enemy trench at M 10 B 4 ½, 8. No 2 gun fired eight rounds on enemy front line range 280 yards, this gun fired on this occasion on enemy line opposite H 31 (British) trench & good results were observed. 9th Rifle Brigade to the right sector & 5th Ox & Bucks K.I. to the left. Infantry relief took place.	Geo.C. Sharpe 1/Lt 4/7 MKR

Army Form C. 2118.

WAR DIARY
or
INTELLIGENCE SUMMARY

(Erase heading not required.)

Instructions regarding War Diaries and Intelligence Summaries are contained in F. S. Regs., Part II. and the Staff Manual respectively. Title Pages will be prepared in manuscript.

Place	Date	Hour	Summary of Events and Information	Remarks and references to Appendices
ARRAS	22.4.16		Eighteen rounds in all were fired from STOKES' guns. Nine from each gun. No 2 gun sustained one "blind." Several rounds were reported by Infantry Officers observing to fall into the German trench, always a desirable occurrence but not too easy to obtain with any degree of regularity.	
	23.4.16		None of our mortars were called on to fire, & the enemy was phenomenally quiet though the battery was bright, and numerous observation balloons were visible.	
	24.4.16		No 1 gun did not fire. No 2 gun fired four rounds on loopholed enemy parapet opposite our salient H.33, with excellent results. The enemy's heavy artillery was very active & H.35 was thrown in by 5.9 shells. In order to provide against the possibility of a German night raid STOKES gun and ammunition was placed in position in H.S line at point M.4, 13.2, 7, covering Ronville - Beaurains road. No such raid took place, & the. the third STOKES gun in line was placed in a day out as reserve gun.	
	25.4.16		A quiet day. No rounds fired by Battery.	
	26.4.16		11 rounds fired by No 2 gun upon enemy trenches at pt. M.4.D.6.6. with good results. hand rounds from No 1 gun & enemy line 200 yds right of Achicourt Beaurains Rd. & all exploded.	

Geo. B. Murphy 2/Lt 2/Lt R.W.A

Army Form C. 2118.

WAR DIARY
or
INTELLIGENCE SUMMARY

(Erase heading not required.)

Instructions regarding War Diaries and Intelligence Summaries are contained in F. S. Regs., Part II. and the Staff Manual respectively. Title Pages will be prepared in manuscript.

Place	Date	Hour	Summary of Events and Information	Remarks and references to Appendices
ARRAS	27.4.16		Organised shoot on enemy loopholes opposite H.34 trench. Stokes battery co-operated with Y.14 medium T.M. Battery & with 4 2/1 T.M. Battery. 5 rounds fired from No 1 gun; 9 rounds fired by No 2 gun upon enemy trenches at pt. M4, D.6, 6. No 3 gun at pt. M4, D1, 9 fired 22 rounds upon enemy loopholes in enemy trench from M4, D.6, 10 to M.4, D.6, 7. These were effective many direct hits on objective being observed.	
	28.4.16		Six rounds were fired from No 1 gun, while No 2 fired two rounds. No "Hund" rounds.	
	29.4.16		A very quiet day for the Battery. No rounds were fired by us.	
	30.4.16		Enemy trench mortars threw "rares" bombs at dark nts our lines at pt. M.4.D.1.1. and a Stokes gun was placed there at pt. M.4.D.½.3.9 this gun fired 6 rounds silenced "raned" bomb thrower. No 1 gun fired one round.	

Geo. B. Sharpe
Lt o/c T.M.B.

Army Form C. 2118.

WAR DIARY
or
INTELLIGENCE SUMMARY
(Erase heading not required.)

Instructions regarding War Diaries and Intelligence Summaries are contained in F. S. Regs., Part II. and the Staff Manual respectively. Title Pages will be prepared in manuscript.

4/1 T.M. Bty

Vol 3

Place	Date	Hour	Summary of Events and Information	Remarks and references to Appendices

WAR DIARY
or
INTELLIGENCE SUMMARY

(Erase heading not required.)

Army Form C. 2118.

Place	Date	Hour	Summary of Events and Information	Remarks and references to Appendices
Arras	6.4.16		Battery went by bus from SIMENCOURT to LIGNY-ST-FLOCHEL to 3rd Army Trench Mortar School to receive STOKES gun, and to receive instruction in use of same.	
	12-4-16		Battery returned to billets in ARRAS bringing four STOKES guns.	
	13-4-16		Battery remained in ARRAS, & details of their kits were completed.	
	14.4.16		Positions in section held by 41 & 42ND INF. BDE chosen for two guns. Position of No1 gun (14th Div.) TRENCH MAP 51B. N.W. 3. Position of No 2 Gun:- M4 D[...]2.5[.] The battery was divided into teams and preparation made for taking two guns into action the following day.	
	15.4.16		At 8-15 P.M. team took two guns into line. Left section was held by 5th K.S.L.I. & right section of brigade front by 9th K.R.R.C. Guns were dug in & partly took up as initial supply of ammunition, thirty-nine STOKES bombs.	
	16.4.16		At 4.15 A.M. both guns were in action retaliating for light trench mortars, & rained bombs. The latter had become somewhat numerous during the previous week but no more than ten were put over on this occasion due to prompt [struck through] [...] No1 gun fired nine rounds [...] No 2 gun [...] An attempt was made by locals trench mortar thrower from the enemy, but without success.	

Geo. G. Sharp
Lt. & 2/Lt.

WAR DIARY
or
INTELLIGENCE SUMMARY

(Erase heading not required.)

Army Form C. 2118.

Place	Date	Hour	Summary of Events and Information	Remarks and references to Appendices
ARRAS	17.4.16		It was thought advisable to place another Stokes gun in position between points (MAP REFERENCE: Trench map 51B.) M10 C4,4, & M10,A,9½,5. On examination distance from enemy lines was found to be too great. The gun is greatly handicapped by the loss of 130 yards range due to the withdrawal of red cartridge. No rounds were fired from guns No.1 & No.2.	
	18.4.16		A very quiet day. No.2 gun fired four rounds, one of which failed to explode, and No.1 gun fired one.	
	19.4.16		No rounds fired. Relief of teams accomplished without incident. 9th KRRC annihilated German patrol. The prisoner captured reported that in his company most of the casualties are caused by our trench mortars as last fired.	
	20.4.16		The enemy again fired a few vaned bombs, but was quickly engaged. No.1 gun fired one round, & No.2 put three rounds into enemy front line at point M 4, D 6, 6.	
	21.4.16		Stokes gun retaliated for light minenwerfer but experienced difficulty in locating the enemy mortar which was firing. No.1 fired 11 rounds. At however range m/s enemy trench at M10 B 4½, 8. No.2 gun fired eight rounds on enemy front line, that shell like 980 yards. This gun fired on this occasion on enemy line of posts at 31 (British) trench & good results were observed. 9th Rifle Brigade to the right section 9.5th D.H. & Bucks K.L. 15th O.H. Infantry relief took place.	Geo H Sharpe 2/Lt 4/R. Bucks

2449 Wt. W14957/M90 750,000 1/16 J.B.C. & A. Forms/C.2118/12.

Army Form C. 2118.

WAR DIARY
or
INTELLIGENCE SUMMARY
(Erase heading not required.)

Instructions regarding War Diaries and Intelligence Summaries are contained in F. S. Regs., Part II. and the Staff Manual respectively. Title Pages will be prepared in manuscript.

Place	Date	Hour	Summary of Events and Information	Remarks and references to Appendices
ARRAS	22.4.16		Eighteen rounds in all were fired from STOKES' guns. Nine from each gun. No 2 gun sustained one 'blind.' Several rounds were reported by Infantry Officers observing to fall into the German trench; always a desirable occurrence but not too easy to obtain with any degree of regularity.	
	23.4.16		None of our mortars were called on to fire. The enemy was phenomenally quiet though the day was bright, and numerous observation balloons were visible.	
	24.4.16		No 1 gun did not fire. No 2 gun fired four rounds on loopholed enemy parapet opposite our salient H.33, with excellent result. The enemy's heavy artillery was very active & H.35 was blown in by 5·9 shells. In order to provide against the possibility of a German night raid, STOKES gun and ammunition was placed in position in H.S. line at point M.4, B.2,7. covering Ronville - Beaurains road. No such raid took place, & this, the third STOKES gun in line was placed in a dug out as Reserve gun.	
	25.4.16		A quiet day. No rounds fired by Battery.	
	26.4.16		11 rounds fired by No 2 gun upon enemy trenches at pt. M.4 D.6.6. with good result. Half rounds from No 1 gun at enemy line 200 yards right of Beaurains Rd. East expended.	

J.C. Murphy 2/Lt 4/? Y.M.R.

2449 Wt. W14957/M90 750,000 1/16 J.B.C. & A. Forms/C.2118/12.

WAR DIARY
or
INTELLIGENCE SUMMARY

Army Form C. 2118.

Place	Date	Hour	Summary of Events and Information	Remarks and references to Appendices
ARRAS	27.4.16		Organised shoot on enemy loopholes opposite H 34 Winch. Stokes battery co-operated with Y.14 medium T.M. Battery & 2/1 T.M. Battery. 5 rounds fired from No 1 gun, 9 rounds fired by No 2 gun upon enemy trenches at pt M4.D.6.6. No.3 gun at pt M4.D.1. fired 22 rounds upon enemy loopholes in enemy trench from M4.D.6.10 to 15.M.4.D.6.7. These were effective many direct hits on objective being observed.	
	28-4.16		Six rounds were fired from No 1 gun, while No 2 fired two rounds. No 'blind' rounds.	
	29.4.16		A very quiet day for the Battery. No rounds were fired by us.	
	30.4.16		Enemy Trench mortars their 'vaned' bombs at dark into our lines at pt M.4.D.11 and a Stokes gun was placed there at pt M.4.D.5.3. This gun fired 6 rounds silenced vaned bomb thrower. No 1 gun fired one round.	

J.R. Sharpe
O/c 2/2 V.M.B

Army Form C. 2118.

WAR DIARY
or
INTELLIGENCE SUMMARY

(Erase heading not required.) 3.7 42/1. Battery.

Instructions regarding War Diaries and Intelligence Summaries are contained in F. S. Regs., Part II. and the Staff Manual respectively. Title Pages will be prepared in manuscript.

Place	Date	Hour	Summary of Events and Information	Remarks and references to Appendices
ARRAS	1.5.16		There was an organised shoot of 7 howling but 3.7 Battery did not join in, and no rounds were fired by us to-day.	
	2.5.16		No 1 gun fired one round, No 4 gun 2 rounds, No 3 gun fired four rounds, one of which was an air-burst. There has been much less varied-burst rifle grenade activity of late.	
	3.5.16.		No 1 gun fired 10 rounds in direction M 10, 13, 5, 8, (Map. 51 3. N W 3.) Two air bursts resulted, other was results were good, grenades burst three or four feet above enemy trench.	
	4.5.16		No 1 gun fired 24 rounds in reply to rifle grenades traversing left to right of M.1. M 10, 13, 5, 8. at 240 yds. increasing to 340 yds.	
	5.5.16.		A day of activity on the part of the enemy. Rifle grenades, bombs & H.2 95.9 artillery were employed against us. All T.M. Batteries replied, our share being 30 rounds. No 3 gun fired 10 rounds, and No 1 fired 20 rounds at safe heading to MAISON ISOLÉE (M 13. 13. *. 7.)	
	6.5.16		No 2 gun fired 18 rounds & No 1 gun fired 11 rounds at MAISON ISOLÉE Firing was much easier to-day as the enemy gave us less artillery harassment.	

S.B.Slater Lt.
42/1, T.M.B.

Army Form C. 2118.

WAR DIARY
or
INTELLIGENCE SUMMARY

(Erase heading not required.)

Place	Date	Hour	Summary of Events and Information	Remarks and references to Appendices
ARRAS	1.5.16		There was an organised shoot of T.M. line but 37 Battery did not open M. and no rounds were fired by us to-day.	
	2.5.16		No 1 gun fired one round, No 4 gun 2 rounds. No 3 gun fired four rounds, one of which was an air-burst. There has been much less varied-burst rifle grenade activity of late.	
	3.5.16		No 1 gun fired 10 rounds in direction M10.B.5.8. (Map. 51B. N.W.3) Two air bursts recorded otherwise results were good. Remainder burst three or four feet above enemy trench.	
	4.5.16		No 1 gun fired 24 rounds in reply to rifle grenades traversing left to right t.pt. M10.B.5.8. at 240 yds. increasing to 340 yds.	
	5.5.16		A day of activity on the part of the enemy. Rifle grenades, toned bombs & 4.2 95.9 artillery were employed against us. All T.M. Batteries replied, ours being 30 rounds. No 3 gun fired 10 rounds, and No 1. fired 20 rounds at enemy bearing to MAISON ISOLÉE (M10.B.A.7.)	
	6.5.16		No 2 gun fired 18 rounds & No 1 gun fired 11 rounds at MAISON ISOLÉE. Firing was much easier to-day as the enemy gave us less artillery punishment.	

SB Slater Lt
421 T.M.B.

Army Form C. 2118.

WAR DIARY
or
INTELLIGENCE SUMMARY
(Erase heading not required.)

Instructions regarding War Diaries and Intelligence Summaries are contained in F. S. Regs., Part II. and the Staff Manual respectively. Title Pages will be prepared in manuscript.

Place	Date	Hour	Summary of Events and Information	Remarks and references to Appendices
ARRAS	7.5.16		No firing was done by us to-day, and Infantry relief of 5/K.S.L.I. & 9/K.R.R.C. by 5/th Oxf Bucks L.I. & 9/th R.B. respectively was accomplished without incident.	
	8.5.16		In co-operation with all our mortars #2/1 T.M.B. fired 20 rounds. A fresh wind made accurate shooting rather difficult. No 4 gun fired 6, T.No 1 fired 14. Results for reasons stated above were only fair.	
	9.5.16		No rounds were fired by us during the day. We did not join in with Stokes' battery which fired at night. Flash of 3.7 T.M. is rather conspicuous.	
	10.5.16		No 1 gun fired at trench sap leading to MAISON ISOLÉE & obtained good bursts a few feet above parapet over loopholes immediately ahead of sap. Ten rounds were fired in all.	
	11.5.16		No 1 gun fired 13 rounds at enemy trench at M10, B.5.8. No other gun fired.	
	12.5.16		Eleven rounds fired from No 1 gun. There appears to be little for No 4 gun to do in its present position & it is proposed to move it to some place from which it can be employed with greater advantage.	
	13.5.16		A very quiet day from point of view of light Trench Mortars. No rounds fired.	

S.B. Slater Lt 42/1 T.M.B.

WAR DIARY
or
INTELLIGENCE SUMMARY

(Erase heading not required.)

Army Form C. 2118.

Place	Date	Hour	Summary of Events and Information	Remarks and references to Appendices
ARRAS	7.5.16		No firing was done by us to-day, and infantry relief of 5th KSLI + 9th KRR by 5th Ox&Bucks & 1. + 9th KRB respectively was accomplished without incident.	
	8.5.16		In co-operation with all our mortars #21, TMB. fired 20 rounds. A fresh wind made accurate shooting rather difficult. No.4 gun fired 6. No.1 fired 14. Results for reasons stated above were only fair.	
	9.5.16		No rounds were fired by us during the day. we did not join in with Stokes battery which fired at night. Flash of 3.7 T.M. is rather conspicuous.	
	10.5.16		No.1 Gun fired at trench sap leading to MAISON ISOLÉE & obtained good bursts a few feet above parapet - over loopholes immediately at head of sap. Ten rounds were fired in all.	
	11.5.16		No.1 gun fired 13 rounds at enemy trench at M.10.B.5.2. No other gun fired.	
	12.5.16		Eleven rounds fired from No.1 gun. There appears to be little for No.4 gun to do in its present position & it is proposed to move it to some place from which it can be employed with greater advantage.	
	13.5.16		A very quiet day. From front of rows of light trench mortars. No rounds fired.	

S.B. Slater Lt. 4th/1st TM

Army Form C. 2118.

WAR DIARY
or
INTELLIGENCE SUMMARY

(Erase heading not required.)

Instructions regarding War Diaries and Intelligence Summaries are contained in F. S. Regs, Part II. and the Staff Manual respectively. Title Pages will be prepared in manuscript.

Place	Date	Hour	Summary of Events and Information	Remarks and references to Appendices
ARRAS	14.5.16		We fired a couple of rounds to trust fired over enemy trench when two sentries appeared to be firing at aeroplanes. As the day was dull we had not much opportunity to carry out this idea fully. We shall make a practice of it in future.	
	15.5.16		A very quiet day. No rounds fired. Infantry relief without incident.	
	16.5.16		One round fired from No.1. gun in accordance with scheme set forth above.	
	17.5.16		No.1. fired 13 rounds harassing enemy front line. No.3. gun fired 2 rounds wire registering on enemy front line M4 D.6.6.	

SBSlater Lt
4/1 TMB

2449 Wt. W14957/M90 750,000 1/16 J.B.C. & A. Forms/C.2118/12.

Army Form C. 2118.

WAR DIARY
or
INTELLIGENCE SUMMARY

(Erase heading not required.)

Instructions regarding War Diaries and Intelligence Summaries are contained in F. S. Regs., Part II. and the Staff Manual respectively. Title Pages will be prepared in manuscript.

Place	Date	Hour	Summary of Events and Information	Remarks and references to Appendices
ARRAS	14.5.16		We fired a couple of rounds burst over enemy trench when two sentries appeared to be firing at aeroplanes. As the day was dull we had not much opportunity to carry out this idea fully. We shall make a practice of it in future.	
	15.5.16		A very quiet day. No rounds fired. Infantry relief without incident.	
	16.5.16		One round fired from No 1. gun in accordance with scheme set forth above.	
	17.5.16		No 1 fired 13 rounds traversing enemy front line. No 3. gun fired 2 rounds registering on enemy front line M4. D.6.6.	

GBSlad... L+
17/5/16 TMB

Army Form C. 2118.

WAR DIARY
or
INTELLIGENCE SUMMARY
(Erase heading not required.)

Place	Date	Hour	Summary of Events and Information	Remarks and references to Appendices
ARRAS	18-5-16		Nothing done by us	
	19-5-16		No 1 gun, which has a greatly improved position on the site of its former one, fired 40 rounds. The other guns did not fire.	
	20-5-16		24 rounds fired by No 1 in reply to rifle grenades	
	21-5-16		No 1 gun fired 16 rounds, and one failed to explode	
	22-5-16		The 3.7 battery fired only 6 rounds, although Stokes' & our other mortars had a fairly busy day.	
	23-5-16		No incidents to report, no firing done by us	
	24-5-16		A yesterday a quiet day, with no firing	
	25-5-16		Our guns No 1 & No 3 fired vigorously. Left gun No 3 fired 30 rounds, & No 1. 10. No blind rounds were sustained and this was very adequate retaliation for enemy projectiles.	
	26-5-16		No 1 fired 6 rounds bursting over enemy front line parapet while Germans were firing at our aeroplanes	

SBSlater Lt
42/1 TMB

Army Form C. 2118.

WAR DIARY
or
INTELLIGENCE SUMMARY

(Erase heading not required.)

Instructions regarding War Diaries and Intelligence Summaries are contained in F. S. Regs., Part II. and the Staff Manual respectively. Title Pages will be prepared in manuscript.

Place	Date	Hour	Summary of Events and Information	Remarks and references to Appendices
ARRAS	18-5-16		Nothing done by us.	
	19-5-16		No 1 gun, which has a greatly improved position on the site of its former one, fired 40 rounds. The other guns did not fire.	
	20-5-16		24 rounds fired by No 1. in reply to rifle grenades.	
	21-5-16		No 1. gun fired 16 rounds, and one failed to explode.	
	22-5-16		The 3.7 battery fired only 6 rounds, although Stokes & our other mortars had a fairly busy day.	
	23-5-16		No incidents to report, no firing done by us.	
	24-5-16		(quiet) day, with no firing.	
	25-5-16		Our guns No 1 + No 3 fired vigorously. Left gun No 3 fired 30 rounds & No 1. 10. No hostile shells were obtained and there was very adequate retaliation for enemy projectiles.	
	26-5-16		No 1 fired 6 rounds, bursting over enemy front line parapet while trenches were firing at our aeroplanes.	SB Slater Lt OMB 4/1 OMB

Army Form C. 2118.

WAR DIARY
or
INTELLIGENCE SUMMARY
(Erase heading not required.)

Instructions regarding War Diaries and Intelligence Summaries are contained in F.S. Regs., Part II. and the Staff Manual respectively. Title Pages will be prepared in manuscript.

Place	Date	Hour	Summary of Events and Information	Remarks and references to Appendices
ARRAS	27.5.16		No 1 gun fired 58 rounds, & No 2 10 rounds. These were fired in co-operation with support of Stokes Battery. There were no blinds.	
	28.5.16		No 3 gun fired 30 rounds above enemy loopholed trench at pt. M4. B5. O. 10 rounds failed to explode but effective bursts were obtained with remainder.	
	29.5.16		No 1 fired 24 rounds at various pts in enemy front trench between M.M10.B3.4. 7½ rpt M10 B5. 6. No 3 gun replying to rifle grenades fired four rounds bursting above enemy parapet opposite H.34.	
	30.5.16		No 1 gun fired 7 rounds in reply to rifle grenades. No other guns fired.	
	31.5.16		Left gun No 4. fired 24 rounds when enemy were firing at aircraft. Infantry relief accomplished without incident.	

SB Slake Lt
4/1 TMB

WAR DIARY
or
INTELLIGENCE SUMMARY
(Erase heading not required.)

Army Form C. 2118.

Place	Date	Hour	Summary of Events and Information	Remarks and references to Appendices
ARRAS	27.5.16		No.1 gun fired 58 rounds & No.2 16 rounds. There were no trench mortar rounds. These were fired in co-operation with support of Stokes Battery.	
	28.5.16		No.3 gun fired 30 rounds above enemy hospital trench at n-pt M4, B5. O. 6 rounds failed to explode but effective hits were obtained with remainder.	
	29.5.16		No.1 fired 24 rounds at various pts in enemy front trench between 4-M.10, B.5, 4, M.4 - M.10 B.5, 6. No.3 gun replying to rifle grenades fired from enemy trench opposite M.34.	
	30.5.16		No.1 gun fired 7 rounds in reply to rifle grenades & other guns fired.	
	31.5.16		Left gun No.4 fired 24 rounds when enemy were firing at aircraft. Infantry relief accomplished without incident.	

SB Slater Lt
1/1 TM B

Army Form C. 2118.

XIV

WAR DIARY
or
INTELLIGENCE SUMMARY 42/2 T M Bty Vol 3

(Erase heading not required.)

Instructions regarding War Diaries and Intelligence Summaries are contained in F. S. Regs., Part II and the Staff Manual respectively. Title Pages will be prepared in manuscript.

Place	Date	Hour	Summary of Events and Information	Remarks and references to Appendices

2449 Wt. W14957/M90 750,000 1/16 J.B.C. & A. Forms/C.2118/12.

Army Form C. 2118.

WAR DIARY
or
INTELLIGENCE SUMMARY
(Erase heading not required.)

Instructions regarding War Diaries and Intelligence Summaries are contained in F.S. Regs., Part II. and the Staff Manual respectively. Title Pages will be prepared in manuscript.

Place	Date	Hour	Summary of Events and Information	Remarks and references to Appendices
ARRAS	1.5.16		Battery fired 12 rounds from No1 gun & 11 from No 3. This was done in Co-operation with V 14 hedium T.M. B and in accordance with an organised shoot supported by artillery. The object was to draw the enemy medium minenwerfer, so that he might be engaged by the artillery. The results obtained were highly successful.	
	2.5.16.		No 3 gun fired 12 rounds & No1 fired 8 rounds.	
	3.5.16		No1 gun fired 5 rounds at pt. M 10. B. 6, 8. (In map 51 B: N.W. 3.) No 2 gun fired 5 rounds traversing enemy front line & left of pt. M 4. D. 6, 3½.	sap kineth
	4.5.16		No 2 gun replying to enemy varied bombs fired five rounds at leading B house at pt. M 4. B. 51, two of which unfortunately failed to explode. No1 fired 10 obsame target as previous day.	
	5.5.16		No 3 gun fired 14 rounds at enemy front line trench M 4. D 5, 9¾. No 1 gun at 300 yds range fired at M 10. B 4½, 7½.: 12 rounds. much hostile artillery & mortar activity in retaliation to which all the Brigade Trench Mortar Batteries Co operated.	
	6.5.16		No 2 gun fired 15 rounds in reply to hostile minenwerfer at enemy front line towards pt M 4. D 5, 5½. No 1 gun fired 28 rounds at enemy front line of hoeuli H 29 traversing from left to right. 43 rounds fired in all & no blinds were observed.	

Army Form C. 2118.

WAR DIARY
or
INTELLIGENCE SUMMARY
(Erase heading not required.)

Instructions regarding War Diaries and Intelligence Summaries are contained in F. S. Regs., Part II. and the Staff Manual respectively. Title Pages will be prepared in manuscript.

Place	Date	Hour	Summary of Events and Information	Remarks and references to Appendices
ARRAS	7.5.16		A very quiet day nothing at all by our mortars. Infantry relief took place without incident. 5th Ox & Bucks L.I. & 9th R.B. are now in front line.	
	8.5.16		An organised shoot was carried out by Artillery and Trench mortars. Stokes fired with two guns at pts. M4.B.6½.0. & M4.D.6.4.½. No 1 gun Right hand gun of these two firing at the latter point fired 12 rounds. Left gun fired 24 rounds. The wind was rather high and therefore accurate shooting with the Stokes was difficult. Several rounds however were observed to fall directly into the enemy trench.	
	9.5.16		10 rounds fired in the early part of day but at 8 p.m. rifle grenades were sent over apparently from Maison Isolée (M.10.C.3.7) & we replied with fifteen rounds Stokes this effectively stopped the trouble but enemy replied with field guns.	
	10.5.16		No 1 gun fired 6 rounds. No 2 gun fired 10 rounds. The latter fired into Maison Isolée & sap leading to same	
	11.5.16		Stokes fired 13 rounds into MAISON ISOLÉE between rounds fired by 6" How. which was shooting at that target at the time. Good results were obtained and nothing occurred. No 2 gun fired 17 rounds at enemy loopholes at pts M4.D.5.6. with excellent effect.	
	12.5.16		11 rounds from No 1. & five rounds from No 2 in reply to a few enemy bombs. No third round.	

Army Form C. 2118.

WAR DIARY
or
INTELLIGENCE SUMMARY
(Erase heading not required.)

Instructions regarding War Diaries and Intelligence Summaries are contained in F. S. Regs., Part II. and the Staff Manual respectively. Title Pages will be prepared in manuscript.

Place	Date	Hour	Summary of Events and Information	Remarks and references to Appendices
ARRAS	13.5.16		42/2. TMB did not fire. A quiet day save for a few heavy medium minenwerfer to which V 14 TMB replied.	
	14.5.16		Again no rounds fired. The weather is bad, and this probably accounts for quiet days.	
	15-5-16		No rounds fired by this Battery. Overhead cover was provided for No 2 gun during this period of inactivity.	
	16.5.16		Three rounds were fired by No1 gun in reply to rained bombs.	
	17.5.16		An organised shoot carried out on M.4.D.5.6. by Stokes & V 14.TMB. This was highly successful. Stokes fired 40 rounds, with one thousand round, and direction length were exceedingly good.	
	18.5.16		No firing by us. A very quiet day.	

Army Form C. 2118.

WAR DIARY
or
INTELLIGENCE SUMMARY

(Erase heading not required.)

Instructions regarding War Diaries and Intelligence Summaries are contained in F. S. Regs., Part II. and the Staff Manual respectively. Title Pages will be prepared in manuscript.

Place	Date	Hour	Summary of Events and Information	Remarks and references to Appendices
ARRAS	19.5.16		No 1 Stokes gun vigorously replied to hostile projectiles, firing 55 rounds in all. There were two blind rounds. No 2 gun fired 14 rounds traversing enemy front line. Very good work accomplished.	
	20.5.16		No 1 Stokes fired 34 in the early morning in reply to enemy rifle-bombs. No 3 Stokes fired 26 later in the day. We are still greatly handicapped by our inability to obtain red cartridges, & the consequent limitation of our range.	
	21.5.16		No 2 gun fired 30 rounds in retaliation to light minenwerfer & No 1 gun fired 9. The results showed accurate shooting as wind was not high.	
	22.5.16		About 5 p.m. enemy bombarded our front and patrol trench in vicinity of Beaurains. Our battery replied to his trench mortars, and freed 25 rounds. Our trenches were slightly damaged.	
	23.5.16		A quiet day for us. The infantry in the line informed a relief without incident. We are busy on new positions for Stokes as overhead cover gives men confidence. Some of these should be in use by the beginning of next month.	

S.B.Slater Lt
for OC 141TMB

Army Form C. 2118.

WAR DIARY
or
INTELLIGENCE SUMMARY
(Erase heading not required.)

Instructions regarding War Diaries and Intelligence Summaries are contained in F. S. Regs., Part II. and the Staff Manual respectively. Title Pages will be prepared in manuscript.

Place	Date	Hour	Summary of Events and Information	Remarks and references to Appendices
ARRAS	24-5-16		The day passed uneventfully, and we did not fire	
	25-5-16		No 2 Stokes fired 29 rounds, & the right gun (No1) fired 15. Of these 44 rounds none were blind, and shooting was accurate	
	26-5-16		A few trench-mortars were fired by the enemy, and we at once replied 33 rounds in all, and enemy mortars ceased. Two guns fired	
	27.5.16		Our artillery carried out a shoot on MAISON ISOLÉE (MID B.3.7) and trench mortars co-operated. Stokes obtained direct hits on say: - & which leading to same. The medium minenwerfer of the enemy which had been quiet for some days, again appeared & replied. H2/2 Battery fired on this occasion 76 rounds (three rounds blind.)	
	28.5.16		Left Stokes gun fired 27 42 rounds, the other guns did not fire.	
	29.5.16		The enemy seems still sore after shoot of 27th again hit-over trench mortars & light bombs. One of the latter dropped in position of No1 gun & wounded the man firing. We fired in all 50 bombs	
	30-5-16		Nil rounds fired	
	31-5-16		No1 gun fired one round. Infantry relief took place without incident.	

Army Form C. 2118.

WAR DIARY
or
INTELLIGENCE SUMMARY
(Erase heading not required.)

Instructions regarding War Diaries and Intelligence Summaries are contained in F. S. Regs., Part II. and the Staff Manual respectively. Title Pages will be prepared in manuscript.

Place	Date	Hour	Summary of Events and Information	Remarks and references to Appendices
ARRAS	1.5.16.		Battery fired 12 rounds from No 1 gun & 11 from No 3. This was done in co-operation with Y 14 medium T.M. B. and in accordance with an organised shoot supported by artillery. The object was to draw the enemy medium minnenwerfer, so that he might be engaged by the artillery. The results obtained were highly successful.	
	2.5.16		No 3 gun fired 12 rounds & No 1 fired 8 rounds.	
	3.5.16		No 1 gun fired 5 rounds at pt. M10 B.6.8. (In Map 51 B.N.W 3). No 2 gun fired 5 rounds traversing enemy front line right half of pt. M14 D6.3½. sap heads	
	4.5.16		No 3 gun replying to enemy trench mortar at pt. M4.B.51, two of which unfortunately failed to leave the trench. No 1 fired 10 at same target as previous day	
	5.5.16		No 3 gun fired 14 rounds at enemy front-line trench M4 D5.9¾. No 1 gun at 300 yds range fired at M10.B4½.1¾. 12 rounds. Much hostile artillery & mortar activity in retaliation to which all the Brigade Trench Mortar Batteries co operated.	
	6.5.16		No 2 gun fired 15 rounds in reply to hostile minenwerfer at enemy front-line trench at M4. D5.5½. No 1 gun fired 28 rounds at enemy front-line & front H.2.q. traversing from left to right, 43 rounds in all & no blinds were observed	

Army Form C. 2118.

WAR DIARY
or
INTELLIGENCE SUMMARY
(Erase heading not required.)

Instructions regarding War Diaries and Intelligence Summaries are contained in F. S. Regs., Part II. and the Staff Manual respectively. Title Pages will be prepared in manuscript.

Place	Date	Hour	Summary of Events and Information	Remarks and references to Appendices
ARRAS	7.5.16		A very quiet day, no firing at all by our mortars. Infantry relief took place without incident. 5th Ox & Bucks L.I. rq'd R.B. are now in front line.	
	8.5.16		An organised shoot was carried out by Artillery and Trench Mortars. Stokes fired with two guns at pts. M4 B.6.2, O. TM4 D 6.1½. Northern right hand gun of these two firing at the latter point fired 12 rounds. Left gun fired 24 rounds. The round was rather high and therefore accurate shooting with the Stokes was difficult. Several rounds however were observed to fall directly into the enemy trench.	
	9.5.16		No rounds fired in the early part of day, but at 8 P.M. rifle grenades were fired against apparently from Hunnin trench (M.16 B.3.7) & we replied with fifteen round Stokes. This effectively stopped the trouble but enemy replied with field guns.	
	10.5.16		No 1 gun fired 6 rounds, No 2 gun fired 10 rounds. The latter fired into Hunnin trenches & sap leading to same.	
	11.5.16		Stokes fired 13 rounds into MAISON ISOLÉE between rounds fired by 6" How. which was shooting at that target at the same time. Good results were obtained and no heavy rounds occurred. No 2 gun fired 17 rounds strenuous loopholes at pt. M4 B.5.6 with excellent effect.	
	12.5.16		11 rounds from No 1. & five rounds from No 2 in reply to a few enemy rounds, no third round.	

2449 Wt. W14957/M90 750,000 1/16 J.B.C. & A. Forms/C.2118/12.

Army Form C. 2118.

WAR DIARY
or
INTELLIGENCE SUMMARY
(Erase heading not required.)

Instructions regarding War Diaries and Intelligence Summaries are contained in F. S. Regs., Part II. and the Staff Manual respectively. Title Pages will be prepared in manuscript.

Place	Date	Hour	Summary of Events and Information	Remarks and references to Appendices
ARRAS	13.5.16		42/2.TMB did not fire; A quiet day. Save for a few medium minenwerfer to which V 14 TMB replied.	
	14.5.16		Again no rounds fired. The weather is bad, and this probably accounts for quiet days.	
	15.5.16		No rounds fired by this Battery. Overhead Cover was provided for No 2 gun during this period of inactivity.	
	16.5.16		Three rounds were fired by No 1 gun in reply to varied bombs.	
	17.5.16		An organised shoot carried out on M.4.D.5.6 by Stokes & V 14 TMB. there was highly successful Stokes fired 40 rounds, with one blind round, and direction & length were exceedingly good.	
	18.5.16		No firing by us a very quiet day.	

2449 Wt. W14957/M90 750,000 1/16 J.B.C. & A. Forms/C.2118/12

Army Form C. 2118.

WAR DIARY
or
INTELLIGENCE SUMMARY
(Erase heading not required.)

Instructions regarding War Diaries and Intelligence Summaries are contained in F. S. Regs., Part II. and the Staff Manual respectively. Title Pages will be prepared in manuscript.

Place	Date	Hour	Summary of Events and Information	Remarks and references to Appendices
ARRAS	19.5.16		No 1 Stokes gun ingeniously replied to hostile projectiles firing 55 round in all. There were two blind rounds. No 2 gun fired 14 rounds traversing enemy front line. Very good work accomplished.	
	20.5.16		No 1 Stokes fired 34 in the early morning in reply to enemy rand. bombs. No 3 Stokes fired 26 later in the day. We are still greatly handicapped by our inability to obtain red cartridges, & the consequent limitation of our range.	
	21.5.16		No 2 gun fired 30 rounds in retaliation to light minenwerfer & No 1 gun fired 9. The results showed accurate shooting as wind was not high.	
	22.5.16		About 5 p.m. enemy bombarded our front and patrol trench in vicinity of Beaurains. Our trolley replied. Whig trench mortars and fired 25 rounds. Our trenches were slightly damaged.	
	23.5.16		A quiet day tio us. The Infantry in the line have performed a relief without incident. We are now on new positions for Stokes as overhead cover gives more confidence. Some of these should be in use by the beginning of next month.	

S.B.Slater Lt.
for O.C. 12th TMB

Army Form C. 2118.

WAR DIARY
or
INTELLIGENCE SUMMARY

(Erase heading not required.)

Place	Date	Hour	Summary of Events and Information	Remarks and references to Appendices
ARRAS	24-5-16		The day passed uneventfully, and we did not fire.	
	25-5-16		No 2 Stokes fired 29 rounds. The light gun (No1) fired 15. Of these 44 rounds none were blind, and shooting was accurate.	
	26-5-16		A few trench mortars were fired by the enemy, and we at once killed two guns fired 33 rounds in all, and enemy mortars ceased.	
	27-5-16		Our artillery carried out a shoot on MAISON ISOLÉE (M10.B.3.7) and trench mortars co-operated. Stokes obtained a direct hit on top. A trench leading towards the medium minenwerfer of the enemy which had been quiet for some days, again appeared & replied. No 2 battery fired on this occasion 76 rounds. (Three rounds blind.)	
	28-5-16		Light Stokes gun fired 42 rounds. The other guns did not fire.	
	29-5-16		The enemy seems still sore after shoot of 27th. Again minenwerfer mortars flight towers. One of the latter dropped in position of No1 gun & wounded the man firing. We fired in all 50 rounds.	
	30-5-16		Nil rounds fired.	
	31-5-16		No1 gun fired one round. Infantry relief took place without incident.	

Army Form C. 2118.

WAR DIARY
or
INTELLIGENCE SUMMARY

(Erase heading not required.)

42/2 STOKES TMB

Place	Date	Hour	Summary of Events and Information	Remarks and references to Appendices
ARRAS	1-6-16		A quiet day. No firing at all. The teams worked on new positions.	
	2-6-16		This morning at 9-30am. The enemy sentrover ranged trench and trench mortars on H 29 & H 30. We fired 30 rounds from No 1. gun and 12 from No 2 gun. Good work was done, and by 10-30am enemy had ceased fire.	
	3-6-16		A reasonably quiet period which we devoted to the preparation of new positions.	
	4-6-16			
	5-6-16		On the 7th one registering round was fired from a new position at M 10 & 2. 3. (MAP S1B NW 3.) but this position has not permanently employed.	
	6-6-16			
	7-6-16		fired 12 rounds	
	8-6-16			
	9-6-16		But No 1 gun in reply to slight minenwerfer attacked bombs. No 2 gun was more active and obtained good results firing 30 rounds in all.	
	10-6-16		No 1. gun fired 15 rounds bearing from M 10. & 3. 6½. to M 10. 6.4. (MAP S1B) No 2 gun fired 12 rounds. This was in co-operation with 6" Howitzine field guns and medium trench mortars. The combined shoot appeared to be most effective.	

SB Chaplin Lt.
for OC 42/2 TMB.

Army Form C. 2118.

WAR DIARY
or
INTELLIGENCE SUMMARY
(Erase heading not required.)

Instructions regarding War Diaries and Intelligence Summaries are contained in F. S. Regs., Part II. and the Staff Manual respectively. Title Pages will be prepared in manuscript.

Place	Date	Hour	Summary of Events and Information	Remarks and references to Appendices
Avan.	11-6-16		The enemy put over heavy flight trench mortars and our No 1 gun fired on new target (M10, b4, 9½) fired 6 rounds. No 2 gun fired 23 rounds at M4, d, 5½, 3½. No (fuzed) rounds were observed.	
	12-6-16		It found ...difficulty as much because enemy was harassing. Result no because	
	13-6-16		going to ...worse protecting in our line we were not desirous of	
	14-6-16		... ...fiercely for the working parties	
	15-6-16			
	16-6-16			
	17-6-16			
	18-6-16		No 1 gun fired 10 + No 2 gun fired 3. The enemy took advantage of our line of ...... to put over trench mortars he replied as above	
	19-6-16		no rounds fired	
	20-6-16		In reply to enemy rifle grenades we took the opportunity to fire 3 registering rounds from new position at point M4 D 1, 5 ½.	
	21-6-16		Nothing to report	
	22-6-16			
	23-6-16		No 2 gun obtained for a few seconds observed bursts, will 2 rounds & fired on an excellent register into enemy trench from M4, d 5½, 4 to M4 d 6½, 2½	SRS Lat 4 hrs 6.6 412/r. TM/13

WAR DIARY
or
INTELLIGENCE SUMMARY

(Erase heading not required.)

Army Form C. 2118.

Place	Date	Hour	Summary of Events and Information	Remarks and references to Appendices
Mons	24-6-16		Took in front line being completed & the enemy again losing blondies we replied with 49 rounds scoring many direct hits on enemy front trench. He did not reply to the following day.	
	25-6-16		No rounds fired	
	26-6-16		Twenty rounds were fired by us. No blind rounds were reported for the day.	
	27-6-16		W.Bom between our accessory, and our artillery trench mortars & 3 guns of 49/2 Battery carried out a bombardment. No 1 gun fired from its original position M10, 4, 9 & 5. No 2 from its original position M4, d, 2, 5, and from a new position at pt. M4, d, 2, 5. G.35, C.2, 0. (51B. N.W.3) fired into trench at pt. M.5, A.8, 9½. No 3 from a new position at pt. G.35, C.2, 0. (51B. N.W.3) fired into trench at pt. M.5, A.8, 9½. No 1 gun fired 17 rounds. No 2 fired 146. No 3, 113. We caused entire most successful operation and sustained no casualties.	
	28-6-16		Enemy opened at 9 pm & at 10 pm with hot artillery & trench mortars & we replied with artillery & trench mortars then battery fired 100 rounds.	

Army Form C. 2118.

WAR DIARY
or
INTELLIGENCE SUMMARY

(Erase heading not required.)

Place	Date	Hour	Summary of Events and Information	Remarks and references to Appendices
Arras	29-6-16		We fired on the activity + Nos 1 + 2 guns fired 80 rounds	
	30-6-16		A raiding party entered enemy's trench about point M.14 d.145, 9¾ and fire stores in (?) at point M.14, b.35, 14 (?) at point M.14, b.7¾, 4½ fired for 26 mins at points M.14 d.3, 9.6, M.14 b.7.0 put up a barrage from mounts in opposing the enemy was repeatedly. We are notified from mounts No 1 fired from 145 rounds No 2. 238 rounds a total of Not effective No 1 fired from 378 rounds from 2 guns in 25 minutes	

Willater ?b
OC 117/3 TMB

Army Form C. 2118.

WAR DIARY
or
INTELLIGENCE SUMMARY

(Erase heading not required.)

42/2 TM Bty

Vol 4

Army Form C. 2118.

WAR DIARY
or
INTELLIGENCE SUMMARY
(Erase heading not required.)

42/2 STOKES TMB

Place	Date	Hour	Summary of Events and Information	Remarks and references to Appendices
ARRAS	1-6-16		A quiet day. No firing at all. The teams worked on new positions.	
	2-6-16		This morning at 9-30 a.m. The enemy sent over varied bombs and trench mortars on H 29 & H 30. We fired 30 rounds from No 1 gun and 12 from No 2 gun. Good work was done, and by 10-30 a.m. enemy had ceased fire.	
	3-6-16		A phenomenally quiet period, which we devoted to the preparation of new positions.	
	4-6-16			
	5-6-16		On the 4th one registering round was fired from a new position at M 10, 6.½.3. (MAP 57 B. N.W. 3.) but this position was not permanently employed.	
	6-6-16			
	7-6-16		fired 12 rounds.	
	8-6-16			
	9-6-16		Our No 1. gun in reply to slight minenwerfer & trench bombs. No 2 gun was more active and obtained good results firing 30 rounds in all.	
	10-6-16.		No 1. gun fired 15 rounds working from M 10, 6.3, 6.½, to M 10, 6.4, 6.½, (MAP 57 B) No 2 gun fired 12 rounds. This was in co-operation with 6" Howitzers, field guns and medium Trench mortars. The combined shoot appeared to be most effective	SB Clark Lt. for O.C. 42/2 TMB.

Army Form C. 2118.

WAR DIARY
or
INTELLIGENCE SUMMARY

(Erase heading not required.)

Instructions regarding War Diaries and Intelligence Summaries are contained in F. S. Regs., Part II. and the Staff Manual respectively. Title Pages will be prepared in manuscript.

Place	Date	Hour	Summary of Events and Information	Remarks and references to Appendices
Tran.	11-6-16		The enemy put over heavy light trench mortars, and our No.1. gun firing on new target (M10, b 4, 9½) fired 6 rounds. No. 2 gun fired 23 rounds at M 4, d 5½, 3¼. No blind rounds were observed.	
	12-6-16		a heavy offensively as much because enemy was particularly quiet as because	
	13-6-16		owing to special work proceeding in our line we were not desirous of	
	14-6-16		creating difficulty for the working parties.	
	15-6-16			
	16-6-16			
	17-6-16			
	18-6-16		No.1. gun fired 10 + No 2 gun fired 3. The enemy took advantage of our lack of retaliation to put over varied bombs. We replied as above.	
	19-6-16		No rounds fired	
	20-6-16		In reply to enemy rifle grenades we took the opportunity to fire 3 registering rounds from new position at point M 4 D 8, 6½.	
	21-6-16		Nothing to report.	
	22-6-16			
	23-6-16		No 2 gun retaliated for a few varied bombs, with rounds @ fired on an excellent register into enemy trench from M 4, d 5½, 4¼ to M 4, d 6¼, 2½	SBS Slater Lt for O.C. 42/2TMB

Army Form C. 2118.

WAR DIARY
or
INTELLIGENCE SUMMARY
(Erase heading not required.)

Place	Date	Hour	Summary of Events and Information	Remarks and references to Appendices
Anas.	24-6-16		Work in front line being completed. The enemy again taking liberties we replied with 49 rounds scoring many direct hits on enemy front trench. He did not annoy us the following day	
	25-6-16		No rounds fired	
	26-6-16		Twenty rounds were fired by us & no blind rounds were reported for the day.	
	27-6-16		At 3PM we sent over "accessory" and our artillery, trench mortars & 3 guns of 42/2 Battery carried out a bombardment. No 1 gun fired from its original position M.10, A, 9½, 5., No 2 from its original position fired from M.4, d, ½, 5. and from a new position at M.4, d, 1, 6. No 3 from a new position at M.5, A, 8, 9½. position adjt G 35, C 2, 0. (51b.3 N.W.3) fired mts trench adjt M.5, A, 8, 9½. No 1 gun fired 145, No 2 fired 145, & No 3, 113. We carried out a most successful operation and sustained no casualties.	
	28-6-16		Enemy opened at 5 AM & at 10 AM with hot artillery & trench mortars we replied with artillery, & trench mortars. This battery fired 150 rounds	

S.B. Slate Lt
for OC 42/2 T.M.B.

Army Form C. 2118.

WAR DIARY
or
INTELLIGENCE SUMMARY
(Erase heading not required.)

Place	Date	Hour	Summary of Events and Information	Remarks and references to Appendices
Arras	29-6-16		We carried on the activity of Nos 1 & 2 guns fired 80 rounds.	
	30-6-16		A raiding party entered enemy's trench about point M.4.d.4½.9¾ and two Stokes mortars (1) at point M.4.b.3½.1½. (2) at point M.4.b.7½.4½ and put up a barrage for 25 mins. at points M.4.d.7, 9½, & M.4.b.7.0 respectively. We are gratified from results in supporting the barrage was most effective. No 1 fired from 145 rounds. No 2 233 rounds. A total of 378 rounds from 2 guns in 25 minutes.	

Signed Tr
for O.C. 111/2 TMB

Army Form C. 2118.

WAR DIARY
or
INTELLIGENCE SUMMARY

(Erase heading not required.)

42/1 TM Bty

June 1916

Place	Date	Hour	Summary of Events and Information	Remarks and references to Appendices

Army Form C. 2118.

WAR DIARY
or
INTELLIGENCE SUMMARY   42/1 T.M.B

(Erase heading not required.)

Instructions regarding War Diaries and Intelligence Summaries are contained in F. S. Regs., Part II. and the Staff Manual respectively. Title Pages will be prepared in manuscript.

Place	Date	Hour	Summary of Events and Information	Remarks and references to Appendices
ARRAS	1-6-16		A quiet day we did no firing.	
	2-6-16		Enemy in the morning 9-30. fired many varied bombs. No 3 gun fired 19 & No 1. 6 rounds. The latter found trouble with mechanism & was not able to fire as many rounds as it would naturally have done.	
	3-6-16		Nil	
	4-6-16		No 1. gun fired 8 rounds at M 10. B 3, 6½ with good graze bursts.	
	5-6-16		No 2 gun fired 12 rounds in retaliation for rifle grenades. One round failed to explode.	
	6-6-16		No 3 gun fired 4 rounds at enemy salient M.4, B 5, 9½ (Tr. Map. 51.B - N.W. 3)	
	7-6-16		Very quiet days. No rounds at all were fired	
	8-6-16			
	9-6-16		No 1 gun fired 19 rounds firing from M 10, B 4, 7¾. & M 10. B 3½, 6½. No 2 gun fired 19 rounds. These were fired in retaliation to enemy bombs & light minenwerfer.	

S.A.Slater Lt.
42/1 T.M. Batty.

Army Form C. 2118.

WAR DIARY
or
INTELLIGENCE SUMMARY
(Erase heading not required.)

Instructions regarding War Diaries and Intelligence Summaries are contained in F. S. Regs., Part II. and the Staff Manual respectively. Title Pages will be prepared in manuscript.

Place	Date	Hour	Summary of Events and Information	Remarks and references to Appendices
Linas	10-6-16		Left gun fired four rounds replying to enemy bombs. No 1 gun in operation with our mortars. 9 with 6" Hows. 8 field guns fired 24 rounds into enemy frontline between points M10, B 5, 9 to M10 B 4½, 7½. A successful shoot resulted. We had no blind rounds.	
	11-6-16		No 1 gun fired 12 rounds at observers post about pt M10, B 5, 9. No 2 gun fired 18 rounds at loopholes M 4, d, 5, 7. all were effective. No 3 gun fired 12 rounds at enemy working party. The enemy searched for our position with field gun.	
	12-6-16		No rounds fired.	
	13-6-16		No 3 gun fired 14 rounds in reply to light minenwerfer. The battery is endeavouring to shoot its ammunition off as it is to be re-armed with 3" Stokes on 20th of the month.	
	14-6-16		Nothing of importance to report. A few light bombs sent over on left of right battalion of the Brigade to which our No 2 gun replied with 4 rounds.	
	15-6-16		No 3 gun fired four rounds in reply to two enemy rifle grenades.	
	16-6-16		No 3 gun fired 17 rounds at enemy front line while he was engaged in shooting at our aeroplanes. No 1 fired 3 rounds.	

SB Slater Lt
4/2/1 TMB

Army Form C. 2118.

WAR DIARY
or
INTELLIGENCE SUMMARY
(Erase heading not required.)

Place	Date	Hour	Summary of Events and Information	Remarks and references to Appendices
Arras	17-6-16		No 3 gun fired 1 rounds abspl from which enemy rifle fire on our planes appeared to come	
	18-6-16		Nos 2 & 3 did not fire. Not was able to fire 9 rounds in retaliation for rifle grenades	
	19-6-16		Battery was withdrawn from the line for rearming at 3rd Army Trench Mortar School with 3" Stokes	

S B Slades Lt
4/1 TMB

CONFIDENTIAL.

WAR DIARY

OF

42ND TRENCH MORTAR BATTERY

1ST – 31ST JULY 1916.

Army Form C. 2118.

WAR DIARY
or
INTELLIGENCE SUMMARY
(Erase heading not required.)

Instructions regarding War Diaries and Intelligence Summaries are contained in F. S. Regs., Part II. and the Staff Manual respectively. Title Pages will be prepared in manuscript.

Place	Date	Hour	Summary of Events and Information	Remarks and references to Appendices
ARRAS	1/7/16		In accordance with operation carried out by the Brigade our guns fired deliberately for one hour three guns were in action. No 1 gun fired on M.10.B.3, 6½ fired 100 rounds. No 2 gun fired on salient opposite H.3H. 86 rounds, while the third gun fired 116 rounds, making a total of 302 rounds for the operation. Later in the day the enemy again opened fire & we retaliated normally with a further 99 rounds.	
	2/7/16		Our guns fired 120 rounds normally in retaliation for enemy missiles. Five blind rounds were reported. Fire on Maison Isolée Sap was very accurate.	
	3/7/16		Less activity generally, though in the evening in reply to light minenwerfen were fired 116 rounds. The ammunition is very good, blind rounds being few.	
	4-7-16		The enemy fired many rance bombs at top of old French communication trench B.16. mid. way between Hartley St. & Hardy St. Our gun there had a rough hour but fired 54 rounds replying to the enemy. 110 rounds were fired by our guns to-day.	
	5-7-16		A comparatively quiet day for us. A dozen light mortars were put over by the enemy, and we fired 17 rounds in reply from No 3 gun.	

Army Form C. 2118.

WAR DIARY
or
INTELLIGENCE SUMMARY
(Erase heading not required.)

Instructions regarding War Diaries and Intelligence Summaries are contained in F. S. Regs., Part II. and the Staff Manual respectively. Title Pages will be prepared in manuscript.

Place	Date	Hour	Summary of Events and Information	Remarks and references to Appendices
ARRAS	6-7-16		Nothing of importance occurred, and we had no occasion to fire the gun team dug out certain hitches leading to the gun as they were practically impassable after the recent bombardments.	
	7-7-16		Thirty rounds were fired on 13 V sap from our Helsen gun with no blind rounds. Our other gun had another quiet day	
	8-7-16		Our No.1. gun fired 42 rounds in retaliation for enemy bombs, and in co-operation with artillery during the afternoon we fired from No.2 gun 114 rounds on 15 enemy frontline at foot of V sap, & 58 rounds on 15 enemy loopholes at the opposite H.34. A good days firing, 193 rounds in all, in respect of the fact that rain penetrated two of our dug out stores.	
	9-7-16		Behind the right battalion of the Brigade all was quiet, on the left of the Rouville-Beaurains Rd, however, we fired a matter of 32 rounds in reply to light minenwerfer.	
	10-7-16		Nil rounds fired. Nothing of importance to report.	

Army Form C. 2118.

WAR DIARY
or
INTELLIGENCE SUMMARY
(Erase heading not required.)

Instructions regarding War Diaries and Intelligence Summaries are contained in F. S. Regs., Part II. and the Staff Manual respectively. Title Pages will be prepared in manuscript.

Place	Date	Hour	Summary of Events and Information	Remarks and references to Appendices
ARRAS	11-7-16		An organised shoot was carried out in an endeavour to destroy enemy medium minenwerfer. We fired 380 rounds from our heat positions as follows: 81, 99, 76, 124. Our shoot was very successful, and the enemy's reply was not heavy.	
	12-7-16		About 8·30 A.M. for a couple of hours the enemy sent over trench bombs, medium flight minenwerfer in large quantities. We replied vigorously with 206 rounds. In the afternoon a further shoot was carried out by us at short notice, and we were able to fire a further 143 rounds. This might have been a much higher total had we not fired so intensely during the morning.	
	13-7-16		An important operation was carried out by the Brigade viz. The annulation of an attack on Beaurains front for one hour commencing at midnight our guns fired (1) M5, a 6, 7, b. M5, a5, 6, 5. (2) M5 a. 6.7 vicinity. (3) M4, d. 6-22, b 5-1, 7 M4 d 5-9, b 5: 1-9. Our operation was difficult owing to our having very short notice, and owing to the excessive firing on two previous days. We fired from all our guns 955 rounds. The percentage of blind rounds cannot be given owing to the bombardment, the difficulty of distinguishing our own shells.	

Army Form C. 2118.

WAR DIARY
or
INTELLIGENCE SUMMARY
(Erase heading not required.)

Place	Date	Hour	Summary of Events and Information	Remarks and references to Appendices
ARRAS	15-7-16		No rounds fired	
	15-7-16		Our No 1 gun fired 96 rounds on traps leading to Maison Isolée, and Nos 2 & 3 guns fired 131 rounds on their normal lines.	
	16-7-16		Only two guns fired. This was in reply to enemy trench bombs & light mortars. We fired 58 rounds from No 1 gun, & on left of Ronville, Beaurains Rd. 67 rounds from our No 4 gun. No blind rounds are reported by either of these guns	
	17-7-16		The enemy was very quiet, and we took advantage of this to repair our	
	18-7-16		positions. Two of the latter have been blown in & we are endeavouring to recover	
	19-7-16		certain guns - parts lost.	
	20-7-16		A few round bombs were thrown on the right & centre battalions of our Brigade. For the right battalion we replied with 42 rounds, & for the left battalion with 48 rounds.	
	21-7-16		A quiet day. No rounds fired by us	

WAR DIARY or INTELLIGENCE SUMMARY

Army Form C. 2118.

Place	Date	Hour	Summary of Events and Information	Remarks and references to Appendices
ARRAS	22-7-16		Our gun left of Helen fired 5 rounds. We withdrew gun from H. Section leaving 4 in position to support 33rd Inf/Bde whilst to open H. section on this right.	
	23-7-16		Two guns of this battery went with I section, and positions covering end of Blangy were at once commenced. We found no Stokes gun in this section when we arrived. About 9.30 p.m. enemy opened a heavy bombardment on I section & left corner of I section. Unfortunately our guns were not in position & were unable to reply. Three hundred rounds of ammunition was at once sent up. O. officer & gun team remained with gun in position till daylight. We were not, however, called on to fire. Two new positions were commenced by us in I section.	
	24-7-16		No firing done by us.	
	25-7-16		I section almost completed.	
	26-7-16		In the afternoon the enemy opened a heavy mortar fire on H. section held by 33rd Inf Bde. & we replied with 117 rounds. Officers & NCO's of T.M.13 of above Brigade were with our gun teams during this shoot. The 33rd Inf/Bde TMB. relieved our guns in H & I section on our right, we left two men per gun with the Bde until 4 p.m. 27th inst. Relief was accomplished without incident by 1–30 p.m.	

Army Form C. 2118.

WAR DIARY
or
INTELLIGENCE SUMMARY

(Erase heading not required.)

Instructions regarding War Diaries and Intelligence Summaries are contained in F. S. Regs., Part II. and the Staff Manual respectively. Title Pages will be prepared in manuscript.

Place	Date	Hour	Summary of Events and Information	Remarks and references to Appendices
ARRAS	27-7-16		We withdrew our gun by day from the line & were conveyed by lorry alright to billets in GRAND RULLECOURT.	
	28-7-16		Battery spent the day in billets in above village	
	29-7-16		By march route Battery moved at 11 A.M. to billets in MÉZEROLLES & arrived there intact at 5 p.m. We bivouaced in fields, and all batting ballies in mess.	
	30-7-16		Remained in above village.	
	31-7-16		Moved at 7 A.M. by march route to HENVILLERS & entered comfortable billets there at 11 A.M.	

2449 Wt. W14957/M90 750,000 1/16 J.B.C. & A. Forms/C.2118/12.

Vol 6

WAR DIARY

SECRET

42nd TRENCH MORTAR BATTERY.

1st-31st AUGUST.

VOL 6

Army Form C. 2118.

WAR DIARY
or
INTELLIGENCE SUMMARY

(Erase heading not required.)

Instructions regarding War Diaries and Intelligence Summaries are contained in F. S. Regs., Part II. and the Staff Manual respectively. Title Pages will be prepared in manuscript.

Place	Date	Hour	Summary of Events and Information	Remarks and references to Appendices
FIENVILLERS	1-8-16		Battery marched into village, & elected to bivouac. Day very hot & dusty. All were bivouaced by 11-30 A.M.	
	2-8-16		Training was commenced. Physical training for half an hour before breakfast, and gun drill afterwards until 12-30 P.M.	
	3-8-16		Programme carried on as above. Physical exercises being varied by running.	
	4-8-16		Parades	
	5-8-16		Battery gave demonstration to all units of 42nd Inf. Bde. of Stokes firing. Rapid fire, barrage, air bursts etc. were demonstrated & good results were obtained by the gun teams. CARDONETTE N.E. of AMIENS.	
	6-8-16		Transport of Battery moved to Vecquemont	
	7-8-16		Battery moved by tactical train from CANDAS (5 miles SW DOULLENS) to MERICOURT (S. of R. ANCRE) and marched thence to BUIRÉ-SUR-L'ANCRE, the transport of battery moving there on same day. Battery was billeted in barns, and arrived in billets about 3 A.M. on 8th.	
BUIRÉ-SUR-L'ANCRE	8-8-16		No parades held till afternoon when a foot inspection, no cases of bad feet were found.	
	9-8-16 }		Parades daily devoted to arm. drill, physical exercises and gun drill. Runners	
	10-8-16 }		practised in their duties, and teams trained in rapid digging in, & laying of Stokes gun.	
	11-8-16		Battery inspected and addressed by G.O.C. 42nd Inf. Bde.	

SPSLuler Capt-

Army Form C. 2118.

WAR DIARY
or
INTELLIGENCE SUMMARY
(Erase heading not required.)

Instructions regarding War Diaries and Intelligence Summaries are contained in F. S. Regs., Part II and the Staff Manual respectively. Title Pages will be prepared in manuscript.

Place	Date	Hour	Summary of Events and Information	Remarks and references to Appendices
Reference ALBERT (Contoured sheet) F.14.b.	12-8-16		Battery moved by march route (5 hours) on hill S.F of BECORDEL BECOURT F.14.b. (Reference after margin). Arrived about NOON, and subsequently in company with Bdes officers scouted POMIERES REDOUBT (A1 b 6.3)	
	13-8-16		Sunday Parade Service	
	14-8-16		Some rain fell during night, and morning was cooler. Battery carried on with usual training, chiefly physical exercises, shortspurts, and ammdrill.	
	15-8-16		Nothing to report.	
	16-8-16		Visited O. C. B.Trench Mortar Batty and discussed positions within wood.	
	17-8-16		Wentunto DELVILLE WOOD about 4 AM. Travelling VIA MONTAUBAN ALLEY. LONGUEVAL ALLEY, and returning VIA CRUCIFIX TRENCH.	
	18-8-16		Two Brigades of 14th Div made successful attack. Capturing many prisoners. Battery remained with 42nd Inf. Bde in reserve in Camp as referred to above.	
MONTAUBAN AND IN LINE IN DELVILLE WOOD	19-8-16		Rain fell during the morning, and at 12 NOON we moved up with guns and Randcarts into MONTAUBAN and took up positions in defences of that village with H.Q's at S.28 c1½, 8½. Battery relieved 43rd TMB. at night. On this day, and we put in two STOKES guns at H.6. S.18 b 6½, 1½, & S.18 b 6½, 2. firing on enemy line between pts T.13 a 0.7. & T.13 a 5.8. The guns did not fire during night. (For MAPS SEE MARGIN)	Reference GUILLEMONT TRENCH MAP 20,000
	20-8-16		Invested guns at 4 A.M. and found all correct. Gun-Captain, a N.C.O. was killed shortly after his visit, by a sniper. Guns did not fire, & the day was spent in an endeavour to provide some head cover for team on the gun. H.15th INF BDE are on our left, & 24th Div on our right.	S/3 Lieut. Capt. N.S.L.J.

Army Form C. 2118.

WAR DIARY
or
INTELLIGENCE SUMMARY

(Erase heading not required.)

Place	Date	Hour	Summary of Events and Information	Remarks and references to Appendices
DELVILLE WOOD	21-8-16		Gun teams in the line relieved without incident. An NCO of battery in charge of carrying party was wounded during the morning.	
	22-8-16		42nd T.M.B. relieved 41st T.M.B. in the line, and 41st T.M.B. relieved 42nd T.M.B. We put four guns into positions as follows:- No.1. S18.b.6.4. No.2. S18.b.1.7. No.3. S18.a.9.9. No.4 at S18.a.8.8. No.1 gun was laid on pt. S18 b 3½ q. No.2 gun was laid on pt. S12 d 2.1½. No.4 at S18.a.8.8. No.1 gun was laid on pt. S12 c 4½.5. The relief between two French Mortar Batteries was accomplished without incident. The 41st Inf. Bde took over our two positions	
	23-8-16		41st Inf. Bde are now on our right and 100th Inf. Bde are on our left.	
	24-8-16		42nd Inf Bde made an attack upon German trenches to clear DELVILLE WOOD of the enemy and establish a line outside the wood from T 13 a 4½ 8½ to about S12 central, and thence to the FLERS-LONGUEVAL Rd S12.a.5½.3. and there effect junction with the Bde of 33rd Div. on our left. (100th Bde) In accordance with instructions received a section of two STOKES guns was allotted to each assaulting Battalion, and moved into position on the early morning of 24th at 4-30 A.M. as follows:- No.1 section attached 9th KRRC. to S18.b.6.4. No.2 section attached 5th KSLI to S18.a.8.8. No.3 section attached 5th OBLI. S12.c.4.3. Guns of No1 section were laid on S 18 b 3½ q traversing to S18. b.5½ 9½. These guns did not fire during preliminary bombardment. At approx. 35 mins after zero, small party of assaulting infantry was seen retiring on left of battalion covered by this section and enemy machine guns were turned on them from S18 b 3½ q & S18 b 5½. The officer in charge of section fired thirty rounds at these machine guns and reports silencing them. S.S. Slater Capt.	

Army Form C. 2118.

WAR DIARY
or
INTELLIGENCE SUMMARY
(Erase heading not required.)

Instructions regarding War Diaries and Intelligence Summaries are contained in F. S. Regs., Part II and the Staff Manual respectively. Title Pages will be prepared in manuscript.

Place	Date	Hour	Summary of Events and Information	Remarks and references to Appendices
—	24-8-16		No casualties were sustained by this section during the operations. No 2 Section remained in its position and as attacking troops were not held up these guns did not come into action during operations of 24th. No 3 section knew by the bombardment withdrew its guns to S.17.b.7.7. at 5-55 P.M. on instructions from O.C. 5th O.B.M. These guns were moved forward to S.12.b.4.4. and they remained there until the 3rd line assaulted. Gun team was instrumental in rounding up a party of the enemy about 40 strong who advanced apparently after 3rd line assaulted. One N.C.O. was wounded during these operations.	Ref. GUILLEMONT TRENCH MAP 1/10,000
	25-8-16		At 9-30 A.M. No.1 section laid two guns enemy trench from pt T.13.a.2.7. to T.13.a.5.8½ and sixty-one rounds were fired during the hot shelling opened by the enemy at dark on the same night. The officer in charge of No.2 section was mortally wounded about 2 A.M. on 25th. At 7 A.M. of No.3 section was instructed to take up position at S.12.c.5.5. He found it impossible to accomplish by day but at night dug in a good position here covering S.12. central.	
BIVOUAC F.14.b.	26-8-16		At 4-30 A.M. 43rd Trench Mortar Battery relieved us. Relief was accomplished without incident. Battery marched back at 8 A.M. to bivouac in original camp.	
Contoured Sheet ALBERT	27-8-16 28-8-16 29-8-16		Spent in camp. Guns were cleaned and examined and handles for universal exercises and arm drill held. Men were bathed in R. Ancre.	
	30-8-16		In pouring rain we moved into billets in DERNANCOURT.	
	31-8-16		Entrained at DERNANCOURT at 10-40 A.M. and arrived at AVESNES CHAUSSOY and marched six miles to AIRAINES at 3 P.M. and arrived in comfortable billets at 6 P.M.	

S.F.Slater Capt.

Army Form C. 2118.

WAR DIARY
or
INTELLIGENCE SUMMARY

(Erase heading not required.)

Instructions regarding War Diaries and Intelligence Summaries are contained in F. S. Regs., Part II. and the Staff Manual respectively. Title Pages will be prepared in manuscript.

Place	Date	Hour	Summary of Events and Information	Remarks and references to Appendices

2449 Wt. W14957/M90 750,000 1/16 J.B.C. & A. Forms/C.2118/12.